SUCCESSFUL
STUDENT
TRANSITION

Ruth Sutton
with Kathleen Gregory and James Gray
Foreword by Ben Levin

PORTAGE & MAIN PRESS

Portage & Main Press gratefully acknowledges the financial support of the Province of Manitoba through the Department of Culture, Heritage, Tourism & Sport and the Manitoba Book Publishing Tax Credit, and the Government of Canada through the Canada Book Fund (CBF) for our publishing activities.

Printed and bound in Canada by Friesens
Cover and interior design by Relish Design Studio Ltd.

Library and Archives Canada Cataloguing in Publication

Sutton, Ruth, 1948-
    Successful student transition / Ruth Sutton.

Includes bibliographical references.
Issued also in electronic formats.
ISBN 978-1-55379-342-7

    1. Articulation (Education). 2. Education, Elementary.
3. Education, Secondary. 4. Student adjustment. I. Title.

LB1626.S98 2012   373.12'1   C2012-900720-X

PORTAGE & MAIN PRESS
100-318 McDermot Avenue
Winnipeg, MB, Canada R3A 0A2
Tel: 204-987-3500 • Toll free: 1-800-667-9673
Toll-free fax: 1-866-734-8477
Email: books@portageandmainpress.com
www.portageandmainpress.com

Contents

Foreword

Improving student outcomes across whole systems of schooling is a big challenge. Yet, it has never been more important. Increasingly, jurisdictions recognize that excellent education is fundamental to a satisfying and successful life for individuals, as well as to building societies that are prosperous, sustainable, and comfortable for people. Moreover, quality education is now seen as requiring both excellence and equity; higher levels of attainment in a broader range of skills for more students with less inequality than ever before in human history.

Success in this effort requires action on many different fronts at the same time. No single measure will make the difference. But many elements can contribute in important ways. This timely book focuses on one area in which we know we could do better and make a difference for students – the transition between elementary and secondary schooling.

For reasons that Ruth Sutton explains in detail in this book, this transition is highly problematic for students in most school systems today. Students are moved from one kind of organization to another one that is often very different in size, structures, expectations, pedagogy, work expectations, and social relations. Usually, students are expected to adapt to these changes with minimal support. We put our young people under considerable stress in making this move, and often do so without thinking much about how we could make the transition smoother. Parents, too, are often confused by the transition process. The result, not surprisingly, is that transition years typically show lower levels of student engagement and achievement, as well as higher levels of stress.

We could do better, however, as this book shows – and we could do it fairly easily. Many books on education are strong on identifying problems but not on providing real and practical ways of addressing these problems. Ruth Sutton provides many specific ideas as to how schools can make the transition years smoother, with benefits to teachers as well as students. Moreover, all her ideas have been put into practice in one setting or another, so all can work.

This book is a lovely amalgam of research, theory, and practice. Sutton delves into the relevant research on these transitions and provides substantive but easy-to-understand concepts for organizing our thinking about problems and potential solutions. The five "bridges" through which she organizes the book represent well-thought-out routes to improvement. In each area, she clearly explains the challenges and offers detailed ideas about how schools could address them.

We also hear the voices of students and teachers throughout the book. These voices reinforce the extent to which her proposals, though sometimes challenging, are deeply anchored in the daily realities of schools and the ways in which teachers and students think and practise.

Such a book could only be written by someone with many years of experience and a keen eye for the way schools work. Ruth Sutton has been a teacher and consultant to schools around the world. More than that, she is both sensitive to the realities teachers and students face every day and unwilling to accept that we cannot do better. She knows the barriers but does not accept them as inevitable. Sutton does not blame teachers or students for problems, but neither does she excuse weaknesses that could be overcome with some effort. At the same time, she is never simply rhetorical. Her work is not littered with the *must* and *should* injunctions that characterize so many works in education reform.

Any school can adopt at least some of the ideas in this book, with positive results. Every system of schools should be considering these ideas seriously and adopting a range of them. If every school and system used even some of the rich proposals Sutton makes, schools would be better places for students, and the transition from elementary to secondary schooling could be a much more helpful part of the student experience.

Ben Levin
University of Toronto

Acknowledgments

Ruth Sutton would like to acknowledge all those schools, teachers, and school leaders who, over 20 years, have helped her to understand the complexities of "successful student transition" – in the UK and New Zealand and, most recently, in Canada. She is especially indebted to James Gray and Kathleen Gregory for their help in translating some of her work into a Canadian context, and for their patient feedback and helpful suggestions, all of which were gratefully received and have found their way into the final work. Thanks, also, to Leigh Hambly at Portage & Main Press for her editing, which has much improved the original text.

Author's Note: In this book, the term *elementary* refers to any type of schooling in which one teacher teachers a classroom of students almost all of the subject areas. This includes schools that are described as elementary, pre-secondary, intermediate, middle, and junior high. Occasionally, in specific situations, the term *intermediate, middle,* or *junior high* is used. The term *secondary* refers to the type of schooling where teaching is divided among several specialist teachers. Secondary schools include high schools, collegiates, and (in New Zealand) colleges. Readers will need to consider how their school is organized in this respect, and they will need to be aware of the impact such organization may have on the relationships between teachers and their students.

Introduction

Students' movement from one school to the next, and the impact on their learning, has been on my mind for many years. For three years during my teaching career, I was head of grades 6–8 in an English secondary school. While I taught there, I visited all the local elementary schools, saw students and teachers at work, and talked to the students about their hopes and anxieties around their upcoming move to what they called the "big school." Despite all our efforts to make the transition from elementary school to secondary school as easy as possible, some of the incoming students really struggled with the changes they faced. We reviewed and amended the ways we did business in the secondary school, to meet students' needs as much as we could.

Since that time, nearly 30 years ago, I have been working with teachers and schools from all phases of the education service – first in England, then in New Zealand, and, more recently, in several Canadian provinces. My experiences have enabled me to connect the messages emerging from international research on transition with the practical strategies to improve students' learning as they move from one stage to the next. In 1998, the Ministry of Education in New Zealand offered me an opportunity to manage a special project on strategies for supporting continuous learning for students as they moved through the middle/junior-high years of schooling, between the ages of 10 and 14. When that work was completed, I wrote a book on the issue, *Primary to Secondary: Overcoming the Muddle in the Middle*. It is this book that I am now translating into the Canadian context – a context that I have begun to understand over the past 10 years and more.

The structures of schooling differ from country to country. In England, most students move into secondary school at the age of 11 and remain in the same school until Year 13, which is grade 12 in Canada.[1]

In Canada, the types of schools are more varied. Some students stay in the elementary school building until the end of grade 6, others until the

---

1. The term *year* (used in countries such as New Zealand and England) can cause confusion in countries such as Canada and the United States, where the term *grade* is used to designate the year. The equivalents seem to be: Year 1 = K, Year 2 = grade 1, Year 3 = grade 2, and so on.

end of grade 9, and still others transfer into middle/junior-high schools for grades 7 and 8 or into grade 9, before moving on to secondary school. Each time students move from one building to another, the continuity of their learning is at risk. The greatest risk occurs when students move from spending most of their time with one teacher to meeting with several specialist subject teachers during any day or week. At that point – students encounter more teachers, and teachers encounter many more students – relationships between students and teachers inevitably weaken.

Strategies for encouraging learning progression as students move from building to building in their middle/junior-high years of schooling might at first sight seem to be quite straightforward. It is relatively easy to gather information about students' learning strengths and needs by capturing the information either on paper or in electronic records and passing it on to the next school. This information can then be used to plan effective programming. How hard can it be?

My experience has taught me that the reality is, in fact, complicated. Teachers who are handing students on to the next stage of their learning will see those students differently from those teachers who will be receiving them. These differences of view are not disrespectful; they merely reflect the different contexts in which the teachers work. For example, the criteria on which judgments of students' strengths and needs are based may be different from one school to the next. Information about a student that elementary teachers think is important may not be considered as important by secondary teachers. The elementary teacher sees the same students and teaches them all – or most – of what they learn, day after day. The secondary teacher is more likely to be a specialist, seeing more students in the course of a week and teaching mainly one subject. These differences inevitably affect the ways teachers see their jobs and their responsibilities. The approach to teaching elementary students is not better or worse than the approach to teaching secondary students – just indisputably different. At its simplest, the difference was expressed memorably to me by one of the teachers I worked with in New Zealand: The goal of elementary education, she said, is to introduce the student to the world; the priority of secondary education is to introduce the world to the student. Understanding the implications of these different contexts is a great start toward successful student transition.

The chapters in this book follow a reasonably sequential pattern. In the first chapter, I focus on the most important people in our schools – the students and their teachers. I present four people, two students and two teachers, whose perspectives I have synthesized from countless conversations and experiences over the years. These "people" represent, in personal form, some of the issues that we need to think about.

In the second chapter, I look through the other end of the telescope. I focus on the larger forces at work in our schools, and then I review the conclusions of the most recent and interesting research into issues of learning and transition. From some of this research, I draw the image of five "bridges for transition" that need to be built between schools, to align and then support the continuity of students' learning. These five bridges are:

> **Pause & Reflect**
>
> From your own experience, what do you think are the differences between teachers working in an elementary school and those working in a secondary school? How do these differences affect your ideas about successful student transition from one school to the other?

1. The managerial/bureaucratic bridge, which is mainly concerned with systems and structures in schools.

2. The social bridge, which focuses on efforts to make students feel safe and secure as they move from one building to the next.

> **Quick Tip**
>
> Remember DRIP – "Data Rich, Information Poor." You may need help interpreting some of the numeric student achievement data we have so much of these days. If you are not sure what the data really means, ask someone to explain it to you.

3. The curriculum-content bridge, which deals with the alignment of content and programming between the elementary and the secondary schools.

4. The pedagogy bridge, which is not as concerned with *what* students learn as it is with *how* they learn it.

5. The "learning-to-learn" bridge, which focuses on developing and maintaining the metacognitive self-awareness of our students, encouraging them to become the "vehicles of their own progression."

It is noteworthy right at the start to understand that the last two bridges – pedagogy and learning to learn – are the hardest to build. However, they have the most positive effect on students' future successes.

In chapters 3 and 4, I present the collective views, first of students, and then of teachers. I gathered these views during my research in this area, together with some analysis of the implications of what students and teachers say.

In chapters 5 and 6, I return to the five "bridges of transition" identified in the research. Strategies relevant to each of these "bridges" are presented, not as quick fixes, but as a range of practical possibilities that schools can consider and use intentionally, with a clear understanding of the values about learning and teaching that underpin them.

Successful student transition is a challenging goal that involves and connects some deep professional issues:

- **Professional trust** among teachers and between the different stages of the education service that, together, enables teachers to provide for students, families, and communities and to work toward a common goal. The level of trust required and the need to collaborate in the best interests of the students may call into question long-standing concerns about teachers' "professional autonomy." This is a hot issue for many teachers. For some, it is about protecting individual teachers from undue pressure as they seek to best serve the interests of their students; for others, it is about teachers recognizing that their work benefits from collaboration with other teachers. Individual professional autonomy is quite different from shared professional autonomy.

> **Pause & Reflect**
> How might these differences affect the ways teachers work, day by day? Which of these definitions of "professional autonomy" do you espouse?

- **Mutual professional respect** between elementary and secondary educators. It is essential and cannot be assumed.
- **Clear understanding and communication** about the students and their strengths and needs. We now have sophisticated technology at our disposal, but some of the ways we use it make understanding and communication more difficult. We can use technology, for example, to create numeric data about almost every aspect of a

student's learning. However, what we can end up with is a caricature of the student, far removed from the real young person. Using technology to help young students capture examples of their own learning strengths and needs to show to their next teachers is far more productive of learning than a spread sheet of marks and grades – but may be more difficult for the receiving school to manage.

- **Sound assessment practices** to form the bedrock of the judgments made by "providing" teachers and understood by "receiving teachers." The information we gather, communicate, and use is only as good as the assessment practice that underpins it.
- **The appropriate type and level of support and challenge** for all students. Under the heading of "differentiation," support and challenge have been part of professional repertoire forever.

> **Pause & Reflect**
>
> To make student transition successful, teachers need the following:
> - Trust and respect between the "providing" school and the "receiving" school
> - Good communication between "providers" and "receivers"
> - Effective differentiation, to identify the specific learning needs of the students as they move smoothly from one school to the next
>
> Consider your own school and the "providing" school from which your students come, or the "receiving" school to which your students will go. Are there matters of trust, respect, communication, and differentiation that you might need to address?

All of these tricky matters are fundamental to successful student transition.

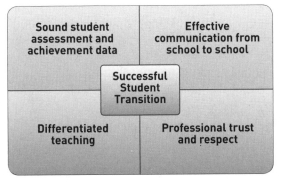

Figure I.1 The Elements of Successful Student Transition. If you were to put lines and arrows onto this diagram to represent priorities and connections, where would you draw them? Can you find a better way to represent these pre-conditions of successful student transition in diagrammatic or visual form?

CHAPTER 1

Learning and Teaching Through the Ages

The title of this chapter refers not to the history of learning and teaching but to the styles of learning and teaching that learners experience as they move through the school system. These styles change as the learner gets older, but in what ways? Is such change inevitable? Does it occur in easy stages or in big steps at certain points in the learner's life?

Let us first look at learning near the beginning of schooling – remembering always that learning is at its most rapid before the child starts school.

Two Learners, Aged Seven and Sixteen
The Seven-Year-Old at School

Sara is seven. She stays in the same classroom for most of the day, except when she is in physical education or music class, outside in the playground or on a school field trip. She works with the same teacher most of the time, too. If you were to ask Sara, she would tell you that she likes her teacher and thinks her teacher likes her. She worries, however, about what might happen if next year's teacher does not like her – after all, they will be together for a whole year.

Two years ago, when Sara first started school, her teacher closely observed her to find out as much as she could about Sara's experiences, her skills and interests, and the ways she communicated and approached different situations. The teacher also talked to Sara's parents about the things she did and said at home, what she enjoyed, what made her laugh, and about her pre-school activities. The teacher passed on her observations and suggestions, both in writing and in conversation, to the next teacher, who, in turn, passed on the information to Sara's grade 2 teacher.

During the day, Sara and her classmates work on a variety of activities, organized by the teacher. These activities are based on what the teacher knows about the students' starting point and needs (including Sara's), and are also influenced by the learning expectations/

outcomes expressed in the provincial curriculum requirements. Every day, students do some number work, and some reading and writing, but there are no bells to signify different periods of time. Sometimes, students continue doing something interesting beyond the time when they usually move on to another activity, and then the teacher reschedules any of the activities the students have missed.

The teacher calls different parts of their learning by different names. Most of the students understand what science is, but many of the things they learn about just merge together. Sara says she remembers a teacher coming from the next school and asking them about social studies, but no one was very clear about what that teacher meant.

Sometimes the teacher talks or reads to the whole class. Sometimes the students work in groups, based on friendship or on the teacher's choice. Sometimes the students work individually on something, and the teacher works alongside each child for a few minutes, to check how learning is going, to make a decision about the next step for the student. Sara enjoys these sessions with her teacher. They talk about what she is good at, what she finds hard to do, and in what areas she has to make a special effort for the next few days or weeks.

Because Sara's teacher spends all of her day with the same group of students, she knows them well, and they know her. The teacher notices things quickly, and, by intervening at the right time, she can often prevent a child from becoming naughty or confused. Because they are together all the time, the teacher and the students develop routines for managing the classroom and the activities. Most students learn these routines quickly. Sara, for one, enjoys the sense of order and security that the routine provides. Routines help the teacher, too, as daily tasks can be achieved quickly and effectively. Visitors to the classroom are often impressed by these routines, which seem to work so well.

The strong bond between the teacher and the students is shared by most of the parents, too. The teacher sees many of them as they bring their children to and from school. Sara's mother often has a word with the teacher on the days when she picks Sara up from school, and she can call Sara's teacher before school starts in the morning if she is concerned about something.

Sara's teacher talked to the students at the start of the year about the importance of working together and supporting each other. She told them how geese fly in a V-shape formation to protect each other and make the best progress. If one of the geese gets ill or tired and falls behind the rest, other geese will detach from the V to surround and support it. "That's the way I would like us to work," she said. "I'll support you, and you will support each other."

In addition to the reading, writing, and math they do every day, Sara and her classmates work on many other activities. They make things to take home or to display around the classroom, which is full of colour and drawings and samples of the students' work. Sara has her own desk where she can keep her things, and her own place – with her name on it – to hang her coat.

Sara does not get grades or scores on her work. Her teacher writes comments about what she is doing well and what she needs to do next. Last year, Sara's teacher gave scores out of 10, and handed out lots of stickers, but her teacher this year does not do that. She once said that she only gives out "Fantastic!" stickers for work that is really special. She expects Sara and her classmates to do good work every day – because they want to, not just to get a sticker. On Sara's report at the end of the year, the teacher will give her a number in some areas of her work so that her mother has an idea of how Sara is doing compared to the provincial standards.[1]

Now, let us move over to the secondary school in the same community, and find out what learning is like for Tom.

The Sixteen-Year-Old at School

Sixteen-year-old Tom is taught by eight teachers each week, in 50-minute periods. Between periods, Tom and his friends move from classroom to classroom, sometimes walking from one end of the building to the other, or even to a neighbouring building. Bells signal the end of each period and the start of the next. There are not enough secure lockers in the school for everyone, so many students carry all of their books with them. Between classes, the school hallways are crowded with students and are quite noisy.

> **Pause & Reflect**
>
> Tom is in a non-semestered school. What will be the differences in Tom's experiences if he is in a semestered school? In terms of good learning for the students, which do you feel is the better way of organizing secondary education?

---

1. These standards are the provincial norms for specific ages and stages of the students.

Each of Tom's teachers has between 100 and 200 students every week. It takes some teachers quite a while to learn the names of all their students, and even longer to understand the learning needs and capabilities of them all. Sometimes, a teacher will teach a group for two years, but more often students have different teachers each year. Tom is not always sure if the teachers talk much to each other about their students, even teachers in the same department, although he realizes there are bound to be some difficult students whom everyone talks about. All the teachers seem to know one of Tom's friends who is very clever, and another boy who is a great hockey player.

During his first year at this secondary school, Tom wondered whether his teachers knew about what he had done at his previous school. Sometimes, it felt as if the students were starting all over again, although some of his teachers clearly were interested in what he had learned before and tried to build on that.

Tom's school week is broken into learning periods, with different subjects taught by different teachers. Tom has math three or four times a week, but he sees some of his other teachers only one or two days a week. Each time, they have to spend a few minutes recalling what they were working on the last time they met. At the beginning of the year, everyone is interested in seeing the timetable, which determines the shape and feel of the week. Some days are definitely better than others. Some students talk among themselves about which afternoons they might be tempted to go downtown, when nothing offered at school really appeals to them, or when they suspect the teachers might be slow to notice their absence. Other days become the highlight of the week, with just the right combination of activities. It is a bit of a lottery really.

When Tom first started at secondary school, he enjoyed the variety of different lessons, with different people and different learning periods, although it was a bit overwhelming and tiring. Every now and then, however, it struck him that the things they were learning in different lessons were connected, although no one pointed out the connection. He had commented to one of his teachers about having learned something similar in another class, and she replied, "Well, this time you're doing it properly," so he did not mentioned it again. Maybe things in math are completely different from technology or social studies, he thought to himself, and left it at that.

Now that Tom is in grade 11, the students occasionally work in groups in some of the classes, and he enjoys that. In previous grades, one or two teachers tried to have the students work in groups. However, it did not work as smoothly as it had in elementary school. In secondary school, each teacher who tried group work had a different way of organizing things, and different ground rules. It was hard to remember who wanted what. Some of the students had thought group work was "babyish," although no one seemed to mind it now. In their careers program, a number of the speakers had talked about the importance of working with others, group problem-solving, and so on. Now, group work seemed to be fashionable again.

Group work is not the only difficult thing to organize when you see so many teachers. One of Tom's teachers expects the students to wait outside the classroom so that he can greet each student at the door as he or she enters the room. Another teacher expects the students to come into the classroom and get to work on a set task immediately.

Teachers' expectations about how work should be presented vary from subject to subject. Teachers use a variety of marking and grading systems, too. When Tom first started at the school, each subject teacher marked and graded work in a different way, some using scores out of 10, others using letter grades, and the art and English teachers not using grades or scores at all. That was okay, but it was hard for students to know how they were doing in the different subjects. More recently, the school has asked all teachers to mark the same way, but there still seems to be several different interpretations of the same codes.

Tom's teachers are a mixed bunch. He hardly knows some of them, and they hardly know him. One teacher regularly calls him by his older brother's name. He feels close to some teachers, especially those he has had for more than one year, and he would talk to them if he needed to do so. When he first started at the school, he missed the relationship he had had with his last elementary-school teacher, but as one of his friends pointed out, "It's fine to have one teacher most of the time if the teacher is really good, but at least at secondary school you don't get stuck all week with someone you don't like, or who doesn't like you."

Tom's mother still gets confused about who teaches what and who she needs to see about various things. At least Tom's homeroom teacher has stayed with the group since they started at the school, and Tom's mother feels at ease and confident with this teacher. At parent-teacher evenings, though, she has to see all Tom's other teachers, or at least try to do so. She often says how different they all are, and what different impressions they give her of her son.

The other striking thing in the past few years has been the impact provincial exams have had on what is taught, how it is taught, and the criteria that are used to judge the quality of the work. The teachers often talk about how all the students will be competing for grades and scores against all the other same-age students in the province. This makes Tom and his friends anxious. This anxiety might help some people to focus, but it leaves Tom feeling as if it is just a lottery, and he cannot influence the result.

Tom is a good student. He enjoys school. He likes the variety of teachers and subjects and the wide range of things to do after school, such as the band he plays in. At lunch time, he often spends time in the school library, working on his homework or reading. He also likes being able to see his friends every day. But he does not feel that anyone really understands him as a learner, except, perhaps, his homeroom teacher, who does not even teach him this year. He wishes there were more chances to connect the various things he is being taught. He wants a clearer idea of how he is getting on, and of what he needs to do to get better grades.

Two Teachers in the Elementary School and the Secondary School
The Elementary-School Teacher

Sahida Chaudhry is an excellent teacher. She works in the elementary school where Sara is a student. Sahida did her teacher training several years ago. From quite an early age, she wanted to be a teacher but was not sure, until much later, whether to teach younger or older students. She decided, in the end, that the elementary years were more important, so that is where she opted to teach. Her parents were not happy about her career choice – they felt she was wasting her talents – but they did not stand in her way.

Some of Sahida's friends teach in secondary schools. They do not understand why she would want to spend her days with young children who need "looking after," rather than "teaching." They all argue occasionally about what teaching actually is, and whether it starts with the student or with the subject matter to be taught.

Sahida likes and appreciates the flexibility and choices her elementary-teaching job gives her. Her days are not dictated by bells and timetables, and she is responsible for ensuring that the week's activities are reasonably balanced. In the past few years, the provincial curriculum has had more influence on what she teaches, but how she teaches it is still largely up to her, using her experience and what she knows about the learning habits and needs of her students.

When she is planning her teaching, Sahida is encouraged to specify the things she wants her students to learn from each activity. The expected expectations/outcomes may be different for different groups of students in her class, and different again for the two students in her room who have "Individual Education Plans" (IEP). She arranges the students' working groups to fit with the needs of different activities and to reflect the learning needs of the students.

When the provincial curriculum was first introduced, all of the teachers worried about the need to cover everything, but now – several years later – they have realized students do not learn everything they are taught, and the focus on learning has re-asserted itself in the school. "Teach less better" was their unofficial school slogan last year – unofficial because they were unsure how the superintendent might react if he knew that the teachers had reached this decision.

Sahida knows it is worth spending time at the beginning of each year establishing the climate and the routines she wants in her classroom. These may not be the same as in other rooms in the school, but the children have a year to benefit from them, and she finds that taking time over this really pays dividends in the end.

Another thing she makes an effort with is the display in her room. She makes her classroom as stimulating and colourful as she can. She remembers how bare some of the classrooms were when she was at secondary school. Others, though, were amazingly different, full of pictures and students' work. In her English teacher's classroom, she still remembers the poems written on the ceiling! And the math rooms had shapes and models hanging from the ceiling, which was one of the things she loved about math.

Sahida believes that a stimulating learning environment and positive learning habits are just as important as the more academic aspects of what she offers her students. She thinks about how children learn, and the circumstances most likely to encourage learning, and that is what she tries to establish in her room. She is interested in math, and loves teaching it, but she knows that math does not stand alone, unconnected to other things she presents to her students.

She teaches the oldest children in the school, in the year before they transfer to secondary school. She remembers what an important stage this was in her learning life, and tries to explain to her students, especially toward the end of the year, what may face them in the secondary school. She still remembers her time in secondary school very clearly. She offers the best advice she can think of to help her students understand what a big step it is into secondary school. "The road to learning is full of potholes to start with," she explains to them. "Next year, the teachers will want you to be running on a smooth learning road, with all the potholes filled in. This is our last chance to fill in your potholes, because next year the teachers will be too busy to help you like I can. Most important, you have to learn to help yourself, because you'll have to work more on your own in the secondary school, and not in groups like you do here. Don't forget you'll see different teachers every day, and you may not know them as well as you know me."

It is many years since Sahida was last in a secondary classroom, but she does not think it has changed much since she was a secondary-school student herself. She wants to encourage her students to treat the move to the next school very seriously. For those who are confident of their ability to take the change in stride, her advice is fine. For students who lack this confidence, Sahida does not realize that she is reinforcing their anxiety about secondary school and their fear that they may not do well there. Her students are hearing similar things about secondary school from other sources, too – from their older siblings and from older children in the community, some of whom think it is funny to warn them about being bullied or getting lost. The combined impact of all this on less-confident children is to undermine their perseverance later. When they encounter difficulties, as many children do during the first weeks and months in the new school, they see this as a fulfillment of their fears, and lose heart.

Sahida is proud of her role as an elementary-school teacher. "I do a good job," she says, "but I can't be responsible for what happens to these children when they leave me and move on. Maybe the teachers in the next school need to examine the effectiveness of what they do. Some of my children come back and see me from time to time when they've started at the next school. Some of them tell me they're repeating things we did here. Others feel lost, and feel that no one really cares about them." She hesitates. "Secondary-school teachers seem to look down on us, because they're specialists in a subject. Well, I'm a specialist, too. I specialize in children's learning. I know that sounds a bit righteous, but I'm fed up with being patronized at best and blamed at worst."

The Secondary-School Teacher

Ben Smith is an excellent secondary-school teacher. He has been teaching for about as long as Sahida has been teaching. He earned a degree in English, then went into advertising for a while before realizing that he really wanted to teach. Now he is head of the English department in a large secondary school, teaching some senior groups and one grade 10 class.

Ben was drawn into teaching by his passion for literature, which began when he was at school, continued through university, was dormant for a while, and then became irresistible. He does not expect to become a published writer himself, but he wants to encourage young people to share his passion. It was always adolescents he wanted to teach, and only English.

When he sits back and thinks about what he is doing (which he does on occasion), the way teaching is organized in the school does not make a lot of sense to him. For as long as he can remember, that is the way teaching has worked in every secondary school he has known. You have a homeroom (if you are lucky), the students come to you, you develop something special between you and the students for an hour or more, and then the students go away again, and another group arrives. The room is definitely his, not theirs.

During his class, Ben focuses entirely on his students, and he assumes and expects that they will focus entirely on him and their shared work. Ben is not particularly interested in what they do elsewhere with other people. English is his passion. He does his best to make it so for as many students as possible. Part of his mission, as he calls it, is to teach his students how to write in all sorts of forms and styles. He is aware that the social studies department also teaches essay-writing skills, and he is not happy about some of what social studies teachers are doing, but it is hard to find time to talk to them about it. Since the school went to a split lunch time to get all the students through the cafeteria, there is no time when all the teachers are together for more than a few minutes. Even after-school meetings and professional development days are so tightly programmed that teachers do not have time to talk to each other about day-to-day things.

Ben most enjoys the time he spends with his older students, who have chosen English literature as an elective, and with whom he can be more himself. Some of them clearly share his enthusiasm, and he loves their energy and fresh views. Each year, he revels in the small number of students who plan to study English at university. For these students, having Ben as their teacher is a life-changing experience.

To some extent, teaching the younger students is, for Ben, a necessary price to pay for the joy of teaching the older ones. The younger students need different things from him, which he is not sure he is very good at giving them. He enjoys teaching these students, but he does not spend a lot of time preparing their lessons – relying on performance rather than planning to hold their attention. He knows this might not be as effective as it could be. He feels constrained by time, and by the impossibility (in his own mind) of treating each as an individual, unlike how he treats his senior students. Every week, Ben sees 100 or more students. He cannot plan for each of them individually, or provide for their enormous range of learning needs. A colleague refers to his younger students as "munchkins," which is affectionate but shows he does not think of them as serious learners.

Ben makes certain assumptions about the starting points of his young students. He expects them to be able to read – for meaning, not just for word recognition. He also expects them to be able to express themselves, in writing, with reasonable accuracy. If they are not confident and capable in reading and writing, he is not always sure how best to help. The school's team of teachers who supports students with special needs is very effective in dealing with children with the most severe learning difficulties. Over the years, Ben has learned a great deal from these specialist teachers about modifying written resources to make them more accessible to less-confident readers. Sometimes, though, he resents having to do this. He perceives his core purpose as literature, not literacy.

Ben occasionally uses groups for teaching, and he always has the desks in his classroom arranged in small groups or in a large circle. Moving the desks and chairs into rows is a form of temporary punishment that he uses until the students show that they can work together sensibly. Ben does not often see areas of the school other than the block he teaches in, but on the occasional forays elsewhere to cover a lesson for a colleague or to find someone, he has noticed that some teachers have the students in rows facing the front all the time. The students in his homeroom talk to him sometimes about the different expectations, methods, and rules that they experience with different teachers, and how confusing it can be.

Ben has always had a homeroom with senior students. He really enjoys his time with them, brief though it may be. He prides himself on the quality of these relationships, and when he teaches any of his own homeroom groups, the bond with those students can get very strong.

For the youngest students in the school, Ben is aware of the information that has been gathered about their prior learning, their skills, and their needs as they transfer into the new school. He believes strongly that the students should be able to make a fresh start in terms of their behaviour and relationships, so he does not want to look at all the past records, even if he has time to do so. On the learning side, Ben knows it would be useful to know beforehand about the patterns and trends of prior achievements among the students, so that he could adjust his plans. But as we have seen, he tends to rely on inspiration rather than detailed planning. Instead, during the first few weeks of the new school year, he gathers information about his students by observing them, and trusts that the real talent will reveal itself in the end.

Teaching programs for the younger students are designed by the teachers themselves, although they – as with their elementary-school colleagues – have to take account of the prescribed learning expectations/outcomes in the provincial curriculum. For the older students, the overriding emphasis is on the provincial exams. Ben is experienced and confident enough now to be selective about what he teaches in depth and detail and what he just skims. His less-experienced colleagues seem very anxious to cover everything, and end up teaching too much too fast for some of their students. "Teach less, better" is Ben's motto, but other teachers in his department are unsure about it. "What happens if there's a big question on the exam on something we haven't covered? Parents will be complaining straight away." Ben's reply is always the same, "We can cover it, but if the students don't learn it they still can't do the question on the exam, and we've not gained anything. We have to motivate first, and you don't do that by covering too much too fast." The argument remains unresolved.

For their first-year students, grade 9, the English teachers tend to plan from an assumption that students will have covered, and learned, all the aspects of language specified in the provincial curriculum for grades K to 8. The only exceptions are special-needs children, for whom special programs are planned and responsibility shared with the teachers providing support. Among the incoming group of students, there will be a few to look out for, usually concerning behaviour, and, sometimes, students who are especially talented in some way. The students entering Ben's school come from five or six elementary and middle/junior-high schools. Despite the provincial curriculum that applies to all of them, the skill and talent of individual teachers seem to have the most impact on what students have learned and are able to do – and there is not much the English team can do about that. They know that it is not really effective to treat most of the new students as if they are working at the same level, but that is basically what happens.

The records that come with the incoming students include grading for each year and each area of learning, but to Ben and his colleagues these marks do not signify very much. Sometimes, the grade seems to bear no relationship to the ability demonstrated by the student at the start of the new school year.

A number of changes and new priorities have been evident in education in the past several years, some of which Ben is very skeptical about. He feels under pressure and defensive about vague but high-profile claims that the quality of teaching and student achievement is not as high as it should be. He feels strongly that he and his colleagues do the best job they can with their students. He has not been trained to teach children how to read, and does not think it is part of his job. If students arrive in secondary school unable or unwilling to learn what he wants and needs to teach them, then it must be necessary to review what happened to them earlier. The secondary-school teachers feel that some of the incoming students are not prepared academically. However, they rarely articulate the details of what that means, or share their concerns explicitly with their students' previous teachers.

Confusion in Teaching Approaches in Grades 6–10

Sara and Tom and Sahida and Ben are not real people: They represent learners and teachers in two stages of the educational system. They are presented here not to represent right or wrong, but merely to show the differences.

The two extremes of the age range of compulsory education learning and teaching reflect different goals and purposes. In the early years, teachers are clear and confident about their aim to introduce the learner to the world. The student is at the centre, and learning is designed to be as holistic and flexible as the teachers can provide. For the 16-year-old, learning is divided into subjects, and teaching is fragmented, too, with specialist subject teaching teams. Each teacher's goal is to introduce the world to the student through the vehicle of his or her specialist knowledge. Such knowledge is highly valued at this stage, and the holistic approach to learning has by now been largely set aside.

The discussion about the various merits of these respective perceptions of knowledge, subjects, and teaching could go on and on, but the fact is that they exist, and in many education systems they are the hallmark of the changes in learning and teaching as the student grows older.

If teachers at both ends of the age range are clear about what they are doing, it appears that somewhere between the two we are faced with confusion. During the middle/junior-high years of schooling, for students aged between around nine or ten and thirteen or fourteen, we may not be certain how best to provide for them. At this stage, students may be old enough to cope successfully with more than one teacher, but they may not be comfortable with eight or more teachers during the school year. They may be ready to leave the relative coziness of the elementary classroom, but not yet be ready to be dropped unaided into the "big school" and to face the "big kids" who inhabit it.

> **Pause & Reflect**
>
> How and when should we introduce students to teaching by separate specialist teachers?
>
> What is the impact of this change on the structures of schooling, and on the successful learning and progress of the students themselves?

***

Having looked briefly at the experiences of the most important people in the education system – the students and their teachers – the focus in chapter 2 will be on the structures and systems that surround their work. We will also focus on what educational research is telling us about the continuity of children's learning. As we do so, we can ask ourselves this "chicken-and-egg" question: Is it the structures of schooling that determine different ways of learning and teaching in elementary and secondary schools, or have the structures themselves been based on different approaches to learning and teaching?

CHAPTER 2

Structures, Systems, and Research

The experiences of the students and teachers recounted in chapter 1 can be recognized in many schools and classrooms around the world. Students and teachers everywhere work in institutions that have certain structures (of both space and time), and are bound by certain systems, many of which arise from the structures they have to serve. Sometimes, it is hard to distinguish the assumptions on which the structures are based, but here are six for a start.

1. Young children cannot be expected to travel far to school. Therefore, elementary schools are relatively small and situated reasonably close to where the children live. In urban areas, where the population is concentrated, these schools may be larger, but they will be within walking distance for most children.

2. The learning needs of young children focus particularly around the following:
   - Learning to read and write
   - Learning to handle numbers
   - Learning to work with others
   - Developing physical and creative growth
   - Developing curiosity

   These basic skills, and others, are harnessed so that young students learn more knowledge and skills, and the ability to apply them. As the basic skills connect so closely with one another, and with the child's overall development, it makes sense for one teacher, working in a single multi-purpose space, to manage the young students.

3. The design of elementary schools follows from these starting points (1 and 2, above), with spaces occupied by teachers who each have particular responsibilities for a group of learners. There may be walls between these spaces, or teachers may share a larger space, but the focus of teaching is usually on each child, with whom a specific teacher forms a close bond for a year or more.

4. As children grow, they become more aware of themselves as part of a wider world. Since the European Renaissance, this wider world has had a tendency to differentiate human knowledge into "specialisms," and to value the acquisition and demonstration of specialist knowledge. Over the past few centuries, the trend toward specialization has accelerated, with consequences for the structures of education.

5. To justify costs, one of the functions of secondary schooling has been to identify and select young people who will benefit the most from the relatively scarce resource of higher education. Schools are asked to prepare those students for such a path. Transition into higher education can be as difficult for some students as transition from elementary to secondary schooling.

6. An ascribed role for secondary schools is preparing larger numbers of young people for the workplace. These students may need a modicum of training to make them more employable. This, in turn, affects the structures of the school and the priorities of those who work in them.

There are other assumptions, of course. One that must be mentioned, although it will not be examined in detail here, is that an effective democracy demands that publicly funded, high-quality education be available for all children, not just for those being groomed for future stardom.

The "Half-Way Hitch"

There seems to be, in my mind at least, some certainty about the purpose and strategies for teaching at both ends of the age spectrum – in the early years and during the final stages of institutionalized learning.

The pursuit of effective learning expectations/outcomes – if this were the only criterion – would dictate that a learner move from one "structure" to the next when he or she is ready to do so, and that there be no fixed chronological steps

> **Pause & Reflect**
>
> At what age does or should the learner shift from one structure to the next? Is there a "half-way hitch" in the middle years of schooling as students move from an elementary style of teaching to a secondary style? If such a "hitch" happens, how should we – as educators – be dealing with it?

to follow. In reality, the pursuit of effective learning expectations/ outcomes is not the only criterion for the design of our structures. In a political process dominated by choices about taxation, the other key criterion is cost, and it is issues of cost and manageability that dominate decisions about structures.

In the various school systems around the world, a huge variety exists in the school structures that cater to students aged 9 to 14. For example, in Canada, each province and territory and even each school district has a range of provisions. Students may stay in elementary schools until the age of 11, or up to 14 in the middle/junior-high schools, or even 15 in some settings. Some secondary schools receive students at the age of 13 in grade 8 or age 14 in grade 9 or 15 in grade 10 – depending on the range of grades in a particular school. Clearly, there is no set pattern, and the range of provision is wide and inexplicable.

Decisions about structures, which in many systems were made decades ago, materialize literally into buildings, which then form the basic infrastructure, expensive both to provide and to change. In addition, the physical structures of education create human structures, training patterns, and career paths, for example, which inspire loyalty based on self-interest, as well as on theories of learning or educational principles. The differing purposes of elementary and secondary education, the physical size and layout of the buildings, and the communities that surround them also create different organizational climates that affect the attitudes and behaviours of those who work in them. Certain ways of working come to appear "natural" and others "unnatural": seeing things from a different perspective becomes more difficult and, therefore, rarer.

In their approach to change, educators often feel inhibited about acknowledging self-interest as a legitimate motivation in a profession ostensibly devoted to the promotion of the interests of the students and their families. But the quality of that service depends essentially upon the motivation and skills of the educators. It would be folly to ignore the motivation of the teachers themselves. If the self-interest of educators encourages or inhibits desirable change, then we must be interested in the answer to the question, "What's in it for the teachers?"

> **Pause & Reflect**
>
> What is in it for all teachers to improve the quality and effectiveness of student transition? Are there any negative implications for teachers?

A Culture of Blame

Any effective examination of differences between elementary and secondary education and the "half-way hitch" needs to be approached without blame. Sometimes blame is directed toward educators as a whole, for their inflexibility or other perceived inadequacies. More commonly, one set of educators directs blame toward teachers who work in different sectors of the education service. Blame grows when we ourselves feel under attack, as a protection against guilt, or for feeling responsible for something that is not going well. If we all felt that all our children were learning and progressing as well as is possible, there would be no need for blame. But the past decade has undermined much of our professional confidence and pride. Educators in many countries and systems have been systematically criticized and blamed for a host of things, from declining standards of grammar usage to the rise in teenage drug abuse. The public has been encouraged to lose faith in teachers, and even if parents have been slow to do so, the indirect impact has been that many teachers and schools have lost faith in themselves.

If we start from the popular (though unproven) assumption that real standards of achievement are falling for students and, by implication, for their teachers, too, then blame will not be far behind. Questioning the effectiveness of others is a perfectly understandable reaction from people who are being collectively accused of incompetence. The problem, however, is that such blame requires others to act, rather than ourselves. Blame can exacerbate the feelings of hopelessness and helplessness that undermine teachers' self-efficacy when they are charged with increasing the self-efficacy of their students.

There are further reasons, too, why schools in different phases do not always trust each other. Judgments of school quality are based more than ever on the quantification of measurable expectations/outcomes, the comparison of these expectations/outcomes with schools in like circumstances, and the attempt to account for the "value-added" by each layer of the education service.

Schools face a strong temptation to react to these pressures in ways that exacerbate the tension between elementary and secondary educators. Secondary schools can point to the poor achievement of their incoming students as a reason for their poor performances later. The interests of elementary schools lie in demonstrating the strength of achievement prior to transfer, which has not been built upon later. It takes courage and confidence to reject blame as an option and to look for more productive solutions.

Recognition of Complexity

If a resolution of the "half-way hitch" problem were easy, we would have cracked it by now. Unfortunately, the issue is fraught with complexity. First, it has to be established, as empirically as possible, that there is truly a hitch in the

> **Pause & Reflect**
>
> Think of an occasion when you have been tempted to blame other educators for students' under achievement. What action might have been possible to turn this anxiety into positive action for improvement?

transition years of schooling, and that this will damage the learning and development of some of our students. Second, we need to accept the complexity of the problem, and realize that a single strategy is unlikely to "fix" it. Third, if it is the case that the main components of the problem are attitudinal rather than structural, then the task can easily slip into the "too hard" basket, and perseverance is required. Finally, the need to review the transition years of schooling can be seen as an opportunity to challenge some of our most fundamental assumptions about learning and teaching, not as a means of beating ourselves up, but as part of what all good learners do all the time – reflect, review, and set goals for improvement.

The "half-way hitch" in our education system, even if it affects only a small proportion of our students, is a window we need to get close to, because of what it may show us about learning and teaching as a whole, during the middle/junior-high years and beyond. The question is not about finding the best age for all students to move from one form of schooling to the next. There never is one right age for all students to do anything. Readiness for change depends on so many variables that it would be fruitless to seek absolute conclusions about the chronology of transfer. What we might seek, however, is information about what happens to students in the transfer from elementary-type to secondary-type schooling, at whatever age this occurs. Can recent educational research help us identify the problem and suggest some solutions?

Why is the "half-way hitch" a useful focus for looking at the school as a whole?

Here is a story from Canada about school improvement. The school in question was regarded by its teachers and its community as a good school, and involvement in a school improvement project was thought to be unnecessary by some of the staff. "If it ain't broke, don't fix it," they said. There had to be focus for the project. It was decided to focus on a group of ninth-grade students who seemed to be at odds with the general climate of achievement. These students, who represented a small proportion of the grade level and a minute proportion of the school as a whole, were falling behind, on the verge of dropping out, dissatisfied, and disruptive in many of their classes. When it was suggested that these students should be the focus of a whole-school improvement project, there was strenuous argument against. Although it was recognized that the school was not succeeding with these students, it was felt that the students represented too small a range of issues to be of interest to the rest of the school. There was also some resentment that in focusing on a small number of disaffected students, the achievements of the rest were being ignored.

Nevertheless, the project went ahead. The at-risk students' circumstances, learning, and motivation were all examined thoroughly. Their individual difficulties were revealed to the extent that the participants were seen as individuals rather than as a group. All sorts of interesting information came to light, which had relevance for wider issues of learning and teaching in all grade levels, not just in grade 9. The outcomes of the project in terms of changes in both attitudes and practice went way beyond the original focus.

One of the researchers involved with the project reported a conversation with a more skeptical staff member. "It was as if we started looking at the school as a wall with tiny windows in it," the teacher said. "From a distance, very little of the view beyond the wall could be seen through the tiny window we had chosen. But the closer we got to the window, the more the view beyond it was revealed to us. Eventually, as we looked through the window, its small size was irrelevant, as what we saw beyond it was the total view. That project showed us things about our school that went way beyond the small group of ninth graders with problems. What we found were problems for us, not just for them, and the spin-offs were much more wide-ranging than we would ever have predicted. It was clear, for example, that most students – not just the small number who were struggling – would benefit from regular conversations with one adult in the school who could monitor their progress, encourage them as learners, and develop a more effective connection with the family. "

Recent Research Findings

Several years ago in the United Kingdom (UK), the implementation of national testing and school inspection produced a plethora of statistical data about the measured learning expectations/outcomes of students at different stages, and the apparent effectiveness of schools' strategies across a wide range of issues. An issue began to emerge about the learning and success of students aged between around 9–10 and 13–14. There had always been anecdotal evidence about what happens to learning and motivation when students move to the "big school," and now the evidence was accumulating to add depth to the research. At the same time, researchers became more interested in the views of the students themselves, sometimes undervalued in the past as too subjective to be credible, and requiring too much time and patience to investigate.

From these two types of sources – assessment data and student interviews – a research team from Homerton College, University of Cambridge, gathered the most complete picture to date in the UK. The report was called, "The Impact of School Transition and Transfer on Pupils' Attitudes to Learning and their Progress." The team's findings were published by the British government in 1999. The authors, Maurice Galton, John Gray, and Jean Rudduck, reviewed all the existing relevant research in the UK and in North America. They included a focus on year-to-year as well as school-to-school transitions in England and Wales. Their starting point was:

> **Pause & Reflect**
> Think about students during their years of transition. They could be moving from a small school to a much larger one or from a school near their home to one farther away. At the same time that they are struggling through puberty, their parents' close involvement in their schooling may be changing. What might be the combined effect of all these changes occurring at the same time?

We need young people who can sustain, through elementary and secondary schooling,

- an enthusiasm for learning
- confidence in themselves as learners
- a sense of achievement and purpose.

The findings of the report are pertinent to systems both inside and outside the UK. The key points are:

- Only a small number of studies have focused on the impact of transition on academic progress, while many more have looked at the personal and social effects.
- Even after allowance is made for the "summer dip" (that is, the effect the long summer vacation has on learning), it is clear that many students experience a "hiatus" in learning after transition. The authors estimate "two out of five students fail to make progress during the year immediately following the change of schools."
- Even when the curriculum is prescribed for both the "providing" (elementary) and "receiving" (secondary) schools to create a continuous learning program between the two, variations in the interpretation and depth of treatment can lead to unexpected discontinuities, particularly in teaching methods rather than in content.
- Some secondary teachers still cling to the principle of the "fresh start."
- In some countries, policies of "parental choice" have fragmented previous connections between schools and led to secondary schools dealing with a larger number of "providing" schools. This is especially the case with single-sex schools in large conurbations. One girls' secondary school in central Auckland, New Zealand, draws students from 75 elementary schools, and this number would not be unusual in many other schools in major cities across North America. It is certainly not conducive to a planned strategy for preparation and induction for each individual student. Even though the inadequacies of "fresh start" are understood, it is a tempting solution to an otherwise tricky problem.

The phrase "opening a can of worms" springs to mind at this point! The research seemed to indicate that there was definitely a problem. Two out of five students "failing to make expected progress" in the year after transfer was too high a proportion to be shrugged off as "natural wastage" or consigned to the "too hard" basket. The researchers did not confine themselves to looking at the assessment scores and performances of students before and after transition. They were interested, too, in the students' attitude to school and the level of "engagement" in their work, measured both by observation and through interviews. From this it appeared that some students, although continuing to do well, were being turned off school after the initial stimulus of transition to the new school had worn off. This phenomenon was particularly noted in the two major American reviews of research, conducted in the 1990s (Wigfield et al. 1991; Anderman and Maehr 1994). The Cambridge 1999 study stated that this research evidence:

1. highlights the significance of transition for students' motivation and sense of "self-as-learner";

2. offers evidence of a downturn in motivation following the initial period of adjustment;

3. emphasizes the importance for students at this age of their school career of social interactions and affiliations; and

4. explains the downturn in terms of loss of self-esteem in a larger and more overtly competitive environment and of the mismatch between students' emerging sense of adulthood and the tendency for schools to regard the new intake as novices.

Not surprisingly, the Cambridge research further indicated that students from the poorest homes and students with existing learning difficulties suffer the most negative consequences from both the long summer break and the transition to a new school, with language skills declining more markedly than math skills. More surprisingly, perhaps, the subject area most vulnerable to the impact of transition was found to be science, where only 35 percent of students were observed to be "engaged" after transition, compared with over 60 percent previously.

From their examination of how schools are currently dealing with transition issues, the authors of the study present five categories of response, which have been described as the "five bridges" that schools can build across the "gulf" between elementary and secondary schooling (Barber 1999). I will explain these bridges here, and then return to them in the final chapters of this book as a means of classifying the wide range of suggested ways forward that have been gathered from our experiences in the UK and elsewhere.

The Five Bridges Across the Elementary to Secondary Divide

1. The managerial/bureaucratic bridge

   These strategies require that school principals in a community or a school district keep in regular touch with one another so that they can provide accurate information about the others' needs and expectations and present their practices to one another. This bridge is particularly useful in communities where the catchment areas of schools are reasonably clearly defined and the number of elementary schools providing students for a local secondary school is not more than a dozen or so. The bureaucratic communication between schools needs to include the records of information about students who move from the elementary to secondary schools. Educators need to know what information has been gathered, how it is presented, when it gets transferred, what happens to it in the "new" school, and so on.

2. The social and personal bridge

   These strategies help students come to terms with their new environment in the "big school." Trips to the receiving school are organized for a good look around and some degree of "orientation" – having students find their way around, locating washrooms (always an anxiety for students), meeting some of the older students. These visits can take place before the students make the actual move, and might involve having them take part in some shared activities, using specialist resources, or attending concerts, and so on. Visits can take place the other way, too, with teachers and students from the secondary school spending time in neighbouring elementary schools. A wide range of possible purposes and activities are suggested later.

3. The curriculum-content bridge

   Provincial/territorial curriculums have been written and amended in recent years with the deliberate purpose of planning for continuity of learning as students move from one school to the next. The research seems to indicate that this exercise – merely writing and publishing teaching expectations/outcomes – has had little impact on the actual continuity of learning. Differences of training, confidence, perspective, and interpretation still have marked influences on teachers' and schools' management of these programs.

Families of schools, which together serve all the children and young people in a particular area, can use the prescribed curriculums as the starting point for some shared planning, assisted by the common language in the headings and nomenclature of the shared curriculum statements. Unless and until the teachers in these schools get into the detail and start talking things through and sharing examples of activities and expectations, the problem of discontinuity remains. When teachers expect to understand each other and then discover that they do not, the task of developing continuity seems even harder than before.

4. The pedagogical bridge

    The three bridges mentioned so far are relatively easy to address, but according to the Cambridge research, the management, social, and curriculum-content strategies appear to have little positive impact on their own. The last two bridges are more problematic, but do seem to make a difference. When the manageable things do not seem to work, and the things that might work are too hard, it is no surprise to find the issue of transition continues to be a challenge year after year.

    Many years ago, a study of teaching and learning in the Inner London Education Authority concluded that *how* children are taught rather than *what* they are taught makes the difference as they moved from school to school. The Cambridge team reached very similar conclusions, and my own study of 11 schools in and around Wellington, New Zealand, also supports the emphasis on pedagogy rather than content. Elementary- and secondary-school teachers do seem to teach differently: the interesting question is whether it is the approach to teaching that has generated different teaching structures, or the other way around. In chapter 4, I present the voices and views of teachers talking about this issue, but one snapshot from those interviews provides an indication of the connection between school structures and teaching methods.

Here is one teacher's view about teaching structures.

Mary is a skilled and experienced teacher in a New Zealand intermediate school (a two-year middle/junior-high school for students in grades 7 and 8). The traditional pattern of teaching in this and many other intermediate schools has been the elementary model of one teacher with one class, although students at this stage go to different teachers in specialist areas, such as Technology. Very recently, and after much debate, Mary's school moved into "semi-specialization" in which for half the day students visit different teachers for some specialist teaching, in teaching periods lasting about an hour.

Mary was fascinated by the impact that this structural change was having on her teaching. "I see these children only for a few hours each week," she said, "and on only two or three occasions, so days can go by in between. We have to spend a few minutes each time I see them recalling what we did last time. I see so many more children each week now that I don't know their particular learning needs and find myself providing only one or two variations on the same task even though I know that some of the children will be struggling or bored. Just at the point where I've got them settled down and I've managed to get round everyone, it's time to pack up. I'll get used to it, I suppose. Many of the teachers like it, because it gives them a chance to focus on teaching what they enjoy and do well, and the children like the variety, but at the moment I'm finding it frustrating."

Mary is an exceptionally skilled classroom teacher who began her career teaching younger children. Her expectations of herself and her children are very high. These include an intimate knowledge of the learning needs of each of her students, and the daily habit of developing activities tailored to those needs. She aims for a high level of "on task" engagement of her students, which takes a while to achieve and then can be maintained for longer than an hour. The schedule of activities she is accustomed to planning in her own classroom is more flexible than the schedule now operating in the school. Under the new arrangements, the end of each teaching period is marked with a siren sound that determines the student's movement from one teacher to the next.

Pause & Reflect

What are your views about what is happening at Mary's school?

It is not surprising that the classroom pedagogy of elementary- and secondary-school teachers is so different, given the enormous variety in the structures of time and space that dictate the organization of teaching. (More about these differences and their implications are explored in chapter 6.) Even so, schools wishing to cross the pedagogical bridge without necessarily changing structures could focus instead on some shared teaching strategies. These strategies could be experienced by the children in the elementary context and then be used again by their teachers in the new school, making a clear and planned link in "ways of working" between the two. Ideally, the teachers will work together initially to learn the strategies and become aware of how these strategies might be used in different contexts.

The strategies in question here may include collaborative group work, task-planning skills, self-correction skills, review and goal-setting, and so on. Many of these are taught and used to great effect in elementary classrooms, but then not used again for a while, or the strategies employ techniques that the students do not recognize. If these skills are assumed or re-taught in the new school, the connection with previous experience may not be obvious to the students, because the new teachers do not know how the previous classroom operated. One might expect that the students will make the connection themselves, and point it out to the new teachers, but there are a host of reasons why this rarely happens. For example, most students in elementary school know how to best work in collaborative groups, but they may not be able to transfer these skills and habits into a secondary context unless the teacher uses similar terminology and strategies to those used in the students' previous experiences.

Serious efforts to cross the pedagogical bridge were found in only one school in 20 in the Cambridge study. Even rarer, in only one school in 50 was there evidence of a focus on the fifth of the five bridges.

5. The "learning-to-learn" bridge

Here, the focus is on learning and includes the explicit coaching of students to develop their own learning skills, both before and after the move into the new learning environment. Students are acutely aware of the ways in which teaching changes as they move from one school to the next – as we shall see in a chapter 3, which is devoted entirely to the students' view of this experience in the middle/

junior-high years. What students are rarely offered is the chance to have these different expectations addressed head-on, with sufficient time devoted to helping them explore and come to terms with the implications of the different structures and methods of teaching they will now encounter.

Think back to the starting point of the Cambridge study, which I mentioned at the beginning of this chapter. An assumption was made about needing young people who can sustain, through elementary and secondary schooling, an enthusiasm for learning, confidence in themselves as learners, and a sense of achievement and purpose.

Examples of school practice aimed at crossing the "learning-to-learn" bridge are hard to find. Some schools arrange for teachers from neighbouring schools to learn together about new approaches to group work or student involvement in assessment, and have then planned these approaches into teaching on either side of the "divide." Some secondary schools devote time in the first months of the students' first year to "learning how to learn at secondary school," explicitly recognizing and catering for the changes the students are facing. In both these cases, teachers and schools have invested time and energy in learning, rather than teaching, in the expectation that the investment will pay off for the students in terms of their confidence and motivation – both of which help in the short term to improve student achievement. These strategies are not alternatives to the pursuit of higher academic performance by the students. Rather, they are an effective means to this end, more effective than simply trying to teach more, faster, leaving the students more passive than active.

> **Pause & Reflect**
> Motivation, enthusiasm, confidence, feedback, goals, a sense of achievement – quite a list! In your school, how do you and your colleagues provide, explicitly and regularly, these essential prerequisites of learning for your students?

***

In the upcoming chapters, I devote more space to the fourth and fifth bridges, because they are less familiar than the first three. Both teaching methods and a focus on learning penetrate deep into the practice and attitudes of teachers and students. They cannot be grafted onto existing practice and expected to work. They do not involve designing new forms, or going to meetings. Instead, they involve the hour-by-hour, day-by-day activities of teachers and students in the relative privacy of classrooms. They are hard to quantify, unglamorous, and do not provide photo opportunities. In the bustle of a market-driven society, they can be, and are, easily marginalized or ignored altogether.

Pause & Reflect

What are the implications of what you have read so far for the way your school and/or classroom works? How might some of these issues be addressed?

CHAPTER 3

The Students' Perspectives and Their Implications

For those who believe that educational research is a precise science, gathering the views of students has always presented problems. Questionnaires rely heavily on the attention the student is able to give to the questions, and the student's interest, capability, and confidence in responding by ticking boxes or writing. Students sometimes weigh their words, both written and oral, less precisely than we might wish. Their responses in interviews may be affected by contextual factors such as the rapport with the interviewer, the dynamics of the group, or the anxiety caused by being talked to in private. The choice of students to interview can radically affect the outcome, as it can with any form of sampling. Objectivity is even more of a problem than normal when students are involved.

Whatever the challenges of gathering students' views, these views cannot be ignored when we are considering learning and the impact that various events and circumstances have on learning. Only learners can improve learning, and only they can tell us about it. We cannot think for them or speak for them. Students must have their own voice, and we need to listen intently to what they are saying.

The Cambridge study, cited in chapter 2, drew on research revealing the student voice and perspective in the United Kingdom (UK) and in North America. To add another dimension, in this chapter we will look in more detail at three southern hemisphere studies. One was published in 1997 by Denise Kirkpatrick from the University of Technology in Sydney, Australia. The views of students in grades 9 and 10 were also gathered from interviews conducted in 1998 and 1999 in the Wellington region in New Zealand. These interviews were conducted by Jenny Poskitt of Massey University, New Zealand, for the Assessment for Learning and Progression (ALP) Project, which was funded by the New Zealand Ministry of Education and directed by me. The third study also emanates from New Zealand, from a study of multicultural schools in the poorest areas of South Auckland, conducted by Jan Hill and Kay Hawk of Massey University.

In the United States, the work of Carol Dweck (1999) highlights how a "fixed mindset" can lead students to fear unfamiliar learning environments.[1]

The Sydney and South Auckland Studies
The Sydney Study

Denise Kirkpatrick's study combined questionnaires with follow-up interviews of a group of students (aged 12) during their last year of elementary schooling and first year of secondary. The interviews were designed to explore student perceptions of the reasons for academic success and failure, which in turn affect their self-efficacy – that is, their belief in their capability to improve. Kirkpatrick was following up on previous research findings: students who attribute success to high effort and failure to low effort generally perform better than those who attribute success to some external cause, such as luck or "being born smart." The difference in these attributions is in the degree of control that can be exercised by the learner. If the "locus of control" for their performance is completely beyond their reach, attributed to luck or to accidental differences between tasks, students' intrinsic motivation declines. Motivation will rise if the learner feels some control over the factors that affect his or her performance.

The most telling outcome of this study is the differences in attribution between elementary and secondary students. Over half of the elementary-school students attributed success to effort. This may reflect the culture of many elementary classrooms, in Australia and elsewhere, in which "trying hard" and "having a go" are encouraged and rewarded. A smaller proportion attributed success to luck, or accidental circumstances of some kind. When these same students were interviewed at secondary school, these proportions were reversed, giving the external causes of performance more emphasis than the internal. If students were successful, they explained this by saying that the task was easy. In some cases, they said, this was because they were just repeating

---

1. Further insight into the attitudes of middle/junior-high students can be found in Rick Wormeli's contribution to *Educational Leadership* (see References).

things they had learned in elementary school. If failure was the outcome, this was attributed to bad luck and other accidental factors. Occasionally, students claimed that getting the task in on time was more important than completing it properly.

All of this is bad news for secondary-school educators. The students in Kirkpatrick's study commented frequently that they had done similar tasks before in their previous school, and that the work was too easy for them. Some students were annoyed about this, as it showed that their teachers had low expectations of their academic capability.

Another finding suggests students attributed success and failure to chance, because they really did not understand the criteria used to judge their work. This might have been because criteria had been explained but had not sunk in, or because the criteria had not been shared by their teachers. "The students commented that at elementary school they believed they had a clear sense of what was expected of them, but this was not clear at high school."

Kirkpatrick suggests some basic steps that can be taken to overcome the change in attribution that seems to coincide with the move from elementary- to secondary-school learning:

- Secondary schools need to examine if there are any features of the school that encourage students to deny responsibility for their own learning, and to see if these can be amended.
- Manageable strategies to this end include making sure students understand both what criteria will be used when academic tasks are being judged and the instructions for successfully completing the task.
- More time is needed for learning and evaluating different approaches to new tasks and problems.
- Classroom environments need to encourage students to see and share the work of others, and to develop an understanding of expected standards.

The South Auckland Study

For some elementary-school students, poverty, poor prior learning, and a lack of academic success in the extended family had already loaded the odds against academic success. Jan Hill and Kay Hawk found that many of the students already understood this, and their own expectations of future academic success were low. Then, in the months leading up to the transition to secondary school, their teachers wanted to prepare them for changes they would face in the receiving school. Students were told that the pace would speed up, the work would be harder, the teachers would be less forgiving, and exams would be based largely on ranking.

However well-meaning the purpose, and however accurate the picture of life in the secondary school, for some students these warnings confirmed their worst fears. Before ever encountering the receiving school, they expected to fail, and would perceive the first signs of difficulty as evidence of the beginning of the end. Almost all students encounter some learning hiccups in the first few weeks or months of the new environment: what matters is how they react to them. Confidence to seek help and a belief that it will come right in the end provide the perseverance needed to get through the problem. If that confidence is already lacking and is now eroded even further, students give up quickly and then enter a downward spiral of difficulty, failure, inattention, and possible disruption from which it is increasingly difficult to break free.

Neither this study nor the Sydney study mentions another "confidence-busting" practice. It may be more apocryphal than real these days, but all of us have heard tales of the secondary-school teacher (or even the principal) who informs the new students (and their parents) that all the students' previous learning counts for nothing – "the real learning starts here." For students who have faith in their abilities, this announcement may be unnerving but represents a challenge they think they can rise to. For students whose self-efficacy is already shaky, this can set them even further back, facing a hill that looks far too steep to climb without the support of what they had learned before.

Pause & Reflect

Why is it so important for teachers to recognize prior learning? What strategies can we use to do so?

The Assessment for Learning and Progression Project Interviews, Wellington, New Zealand

This project involved 11 schools: four secondary (aged 13–18), six intermediate (aged 11–13) and one elementary-intermediate school (aged 5–13). Each school was asked to nominate a reasonably random sample of about 12 students in grades 9 and 10. These students were interviewed in small groups by a professional researcher with specific experience in talking to students and young people. Just a few weeks before the end of the school year, aged 11–13 students were asked what they were looking forward to in their receiving school, what they expected work to be like there, what they wanted their new teachers to know about them, how they wanted to be assessed, and if there was anything about moving to the receiving school that worried them.

In addition, clear trends and so on emerged from the intermediate responses. Students were looking forward to the newness of it all, new friends, new subjects, and new choices. More than half of them said that they expected the work to be harder, with math and science mentioned most frequently in this category. Physical education was a major attraction for nearly half the students. A large majority wanted their new teachers to know about their learning strengths and needs and to act upon them. They wanted to be given work that was "not too hard and not too easy." This was the highest consistency of response of all the questions asked. On the assessment side, the intermediate students wanted assessment to help them do better, and they did not like end-of-year exams. Students were very clear that assessment should help them know how to improve their work and help teachers see how to teach them better. Only a few students said that the purpose of assessment was just to provide information for the teachers, or to frighten students into working harder. Clear trends were discernible about what worried the grade 9 students most. In descending order of importance, three key factors were (1) getting lost, (2) making friends and being bullied, and (3) potential learning problems (especially homework).

For the grade 10 students interviewed at the same time, toward the end of their first year at secondary school, the start of secondary school already seemed a long time ago. Getting lost and making friends, which had loomed so large a year before, now seemed easy in retrospect. But over half the students were very critical of the classroom experience, commenting on the strictness of the teachers, the amount of homework, too much teacher talk, too much writing, work that was too easy or too hard, and having to adjust to different teachers' expectations. These grade 10 students were as hostile to end-of-year exams as their younger peers were, but they seemed to have forgotten their previous ideas about the purpose of assessment. Only five or six students now identified the purpose of assessment as a means to provide feedback and improve learning and teaching. The remaining students either were not sure what assessment was for or assumed it was about making them work harder.

When they were asked what advice they would offer to incoming grade 8 students, the veteran eighth graders were offered these bits of wisdom: keep on the right side of the teachers, listen to them carefully, work hard, do not skip lessons or fool around. They urged a positive and constructive approach to new subjects and experiences, keeping out of trouble, being yourself rather than emulating older students, and trying your best.

Implications

What can we glean from these students' views?

- The students are most concerned, before transition, about the social and environmental changes they face rather than those involving learning and teaching. "Feelings are facts." If those are the students' feelings, then we must deal with them seriously, or expect these issues to be distracting, particularly in the first few weeks or months in the receiving school. A student who feels very insecure and anxious is unlikely to learn well. All sorts of strategies are possible here, and schools are getting better and better at helping with these concerns. Several suggestions and examples can be found in chapter 5.

- Most students are ready to see a variety of adults and encounter a greater variety of learning "contexts" by the time they approach transition to secondary school. However, we should not expect them to cope with major changes in teaching organization and style all at once. It should be possible to plan the transition from elementary to secondary organization by stages. In the final year of elementary, if possible, students might be taught by two or three teachers before encountering a larger number of teachers in the first year of secondary. They might move around to specialist areas but still have a physical base they can call their own, and a safe place to keep their books and belongings instead of carrying everything with them. They will enjoy the stimuli of a range of teachers, but still be carefully monitored and supported by one teacher who has oversight of their learning across the school, close contact with individual students and their parents or caregivers, and a clear role to act as the advocate of the student in dealings with other teachers. If these strategies are to work in a secondary school, they will cut across many long-standing attitudes, systems, and structures. The barriers to change should not be underestimated, but neither should they prevent a more student-centred approach to the organization of learning and teaching.

- Planning for teaching the incoming cohort of students in the secondary school also needs review, if we are really listening to and truly hearing what our students are telling us. They want, expect, and deserve tasks and standards from their new teachers that are "not too easy and not too hard." This sounds straightforward enough, but it is fraught with difficulties. Here are some:

  - The student's previous teacher is the best source of advice about the learning potential and needs of the student. The logistics of transition, however, create difficulties when the new school receives students from a large number of schools. The teachers of all these students have idiosyncratic ways of expressing what they know about the students. For information to be useful, providing and receiving teachers need to talk to each other in some depth to establish what the one is willing to write down and the other is willing to read and act upon. These conversations are frequently frustrating, because the two teachers are wary of each other, rarely understand each other well, and may have insufficient time to work things out between them.

  - Many elementary teachers are convinced that their secondary colleagues will not read information about an individual student's learning needs. They believe, at best, that the structures of secondary teaching do not allow individual needs to be catered for, even if they have been identified. At worst, elementary teachers feel patronized or even ignored by secondary teachers, who – they feel – regard themselves as better educated (because they are "subject specialists") and professionally superior to teachers of younger students. The resentment caused by this can undermine even the most professional approach to gathering and communicating information about their students' learning.

  - The academic snobbery that bedevils teachers' professional relationships is illustrated through many anecdotes. For reasons we can only speculate about, there seems to be a view in some quarters that our intelligence and professional capability is a function of the age of the students we teach. This view is obviously both mistaken and unhelpful in building trust between teachers at different stages of schooling. It can be an insidious and troublesome barrier to the pursuit of a more sensible approach to elementary-secondary transition, and all other transitions, come to that. In recent years, most teachers have become more aware of the challenges faced by those working at stages of schooling different from their own. School teachers in Canada will often have experience in different stages of schooling, and this helps to break down misunderstandings and confirm a shared professional interest in supporting students' learning.

- If information about learning is provided by the previous teacher, it will be several weeks out of date by the time it is read and acted upon in the early weeks of the next school year. It may well be necessary to spend a little time gradually recalling and reviewing learning that took place before the break. If students cannot instantly recall their prior learning, we should not assume that this prior learning has not happened and that the students' records are inaccurate. It often takes a while for students to recall what they learned before and to have the confidence to articulate it.

- In the first few weeks at the new school, some students are quite overwhelmed – by the size and complexity of the school, by making new friends, by the number of adults they have to deal with, by the travelling to and from school, and by a host of other new routines. All this is in addition to the annual re-adjustment to school after the long holiday. Some schools, however, insist that the new students be assessed during the first few days to determine ability groupings for the remainder of the year. To some extent, this urge to "get organized" is understandable, but the validity and reliability of first-week testing is highly questionable.

By whatever means, teachers will discover enough about the starting points of the students to be able to plan appropriately for them. But what if the teaching plan for the first year is already fixed and so rigidly tied to a time frame or to specified resources that the teacher cannot amend it sufficiently to meet what she now knows to be the needs of her students? Or what if the teacher simply does not know how to adapt teaching activities to make them accessible to a wider range of learning skills and styles than she had originally planned for?

Recognition of prior learning is inextricably linked to differentiation – the adaptation of teaching plans to meet the identified needs of individuals or groups of students. This can be a major challenge for the mainstream secondary teacher who teaches a large number students every week.

> **Pause & Reflect**
> What is the point of finding out about prior learning if we cannot or do not act upon the information?

- A further implication of the views expressed by the students concerns the ways they work with their new teachers. The students are used to working with one teacher for most of the time. They have grown used to the methods and routines of this teacher. Communication between teacher and students has become more efficient through long-standing familiarity. The students know each other well, too, and who and when to ask if they are not sure about something.

- Students are now faced with several teachers each week, none of whom they know well or who knows them. The routines and ways of explaining things vary considerably from teacher to teacher. Students are keen to please and to do as they are asked. Sometimes, though, they simply do not understand the teachers' instructions, are unclear about the teachers' expectations, and do not know the criteria by which the quality of their work will be judged. The students we interviewed in Wellington asked that the teachers be more patient and explain things more carefully so they would know and understand what the teachers expected of them. These needs are usually temporary, while the students adjust. Some teachers find it necessary to set strict parameters for clear classroom control, and a "tight start" to the year may be challenged.

  - When students were asked about assessment methods, they said they wanted assessment to give them specific information about what they were doing right and what they needed to improve on. This is the obvious concomitant of their desire to know the criteria, and the two fit naturally together.

- The students wanted some of their learning to be fun, and the teacher to be even-tempered and not moody or grumpy. They did not want to be shown up in class, when they were still not sure about their new classmates and often very self-conscious. Sarcasm from the teacher was most feared, because it could humiliate the students in front of their peers.

- There was a concern about homework. Many students in our sample were used to homework that was designed and assigned by their class teacher, leaving no chance of different homework expectations clashing with each other. Moreover, the class teacher knew each student's capabilities and circumstances very well, having had sole charge of the same students for a year.

All of the students had been warned that secondary-school teachers expect homework to be given and completed every night. For some students, the whole issue was a nightmare. Their home circumstances simply did not lend to quiet study at home. As teachers may be aware, some homes are overcrowded to the point where the student does not have a quiet place to work. For some students, family responsibilities push homework to the edge of their concerns. Some parents believe that school is for school work and home is for the family and the family's commitments – to the business, to older relatives or younger siblings, to church, or to the mosque. Students who face these conflicting priorities quickly learn to react to the strongest pressures upon them, whatever those might be and whatever the consequences of not fulfilling some of the school's requirements.

For all students, life was made even more complicated if they did not know in advance what homework was expected by each teacher, and what the deadlines were. Some schools plan a homework schedule that dictates (or attempts to) which teachers and subjects will require homework on which night, to ensure that the workload is reasonably evenly spread. In other schools, the suggestion of a homework schedule is regarded by teachers as an unwarranted intrusion on their professional autonomy, whatever headaches it may cause the students. The amount and nature of the homework also worried the students in the Wellington study. Many families have experienced the problem of the homework task that turns out, perhaps through a misinterpretation by the student, to be a family problem lasting half the night. The homework task, the same assigned for all the students in a mixed-ability group, is simply too much for some students to tackle without help, and beyond the capability or experience of the adults at home who try to help if they can.

Sometimes, the teacher uses homework as a means of finishing off tasks not completed in class, so that all the students can move on together. However, students who do not finish the task in class and have to complete it at home may need help that is not available to them at home. Meanwhile, students who have sailed through the classroom task and clearly need something more challenging are left with no homework at all.

Of course, it is useful for students to learn and practise academic work outside the classroom, away from the immediate availability of help. But for students in the first few months of the receiving school environment, homework can drive a further distance between those who are coping and those who are not. Much of the difference derives from the difference in parental support for the student at home – already a major factor underpinning the success or otherwise of the student at school.

> **Pause & Reflect**
>
> Is homework an ongoing concern at your school? How might you tackle some of the issues raised about homework?

A Year On: "Give Up or Catch Up"

One of the authors of the Cambridge study, Jean Rudduck, interviewed, for a different purpose, many students in their second or third year at secondary school. At this stage, students spoke of a choice that faces them as the serious business of grades and exams loom large in their senior secondary years. By now they felt quite at home socially. Fears of getting lost had faded, and instead of being overawed by the size of the school and by size of the older students, they were now becoming those "bigger kids" themselves.

Some students began to realize that they were falling further and further behind academically. For a while, early on in the receiving school, they had been too distracted by the novelty of attending the "big school" to either know or care that this was happening. If secondary-

Something to Try

Check your students' views. The reactions of students in schools far away from yours, in different circumstances, may not provide you with evidence convincing enough to try intervention in your own school. If you believe that the students' perceptions are a vital part of the picture, then you may want to check them out for yourself. It takes time to do this well. If it is not done well, it is not worth doing at all. Here are some suggestions from my own experience:

- Sampling: As a rough rule of thumb, involving fewer than 30 students will not give you the depth of information you need. You have to decide whether to take a random sample – say, one in five from the school attendance roll – or to focus attention on a more specific group.
- Choosing a method: Questionnaires are quick and relatively inexpensive, but the design and wording need to be easy for students to use, to provide the information you are looking for.
- Interviewing: Interviewing students can provide more depth and detail, and, here again, careful thought is necessary about the questions to ask and who is going to ask them. Is it better to interview students individually or in small groups? In my experience, students tend to talk more in a group, and respond in greater depth. In addition, group interviews are less time-consuming than one-to-one interviews.
- Using audio or video to capture what the students say: This leaves the interviewer free to listen carefully. Audio tape is less obtrusive. Transcribing can be difficult, but sometimes it is important to hear the students' voices, not just read what they say.

Whatever the form of the questions, their purpose is to improve students' experience of school, and of their learning. When teachers have been able to contribute to the questions, they are more likely to be interested in the responses.

school teachers' expectations of students had been too low, as some elementary teachers claim, and the students were of a mind to do no more than what was required of them, their performance standards would have been slowly but surely slipping away.

When such a student began to realize that he (and this is most common with boys) had a problem, he also had to decide what to do about it. This was where the student's belief in self (self-efficacy) became so crucial. If he believed that with help he could catch up, then he would probably find a way to get help. Often, this would be from other students, but teachers could also pick up the signals that a student wanted to catch up. Other students whose self-efficacy is low may react to early problems by assuming they are going to fail and giving up. Failure at school may be the repeating pattern in the family and regarded as something no one has any control over. "My mom says she could never do math either, and not to worry about it." Parents sometimes collude with these low expectations from a desire to protect their children from the anxiety and frustration of raising their sights, because they suspect the effort will be fruitless, and they want their children to be happy. As parents, many of us have faced this dilemma, and have struggled with it in our own way. In her book, *Mindset*, Carol Dweck outlines what teachers and parents can do to help students develop a more positive approach to learning.

Students with less faith in themselves are often those who decide to give up rather than catch up. They may continue to attend school, see their friends, and enjoy the activities, but they have actually given up. Some students will give up more completely and sustain their self-respect by overt rejection of school and all it stands for. They pursue their satisfaction elsewhere, as far away as they can get.

"Catch up or give up" is a choice many students face when their earlier learning progress has not been sustained.

> **Pause & Reflect**
>
> To find out about students' expectations of the receiving school, or about their actual experiences of transition from elementary to secondary school, what questions would you ask them?

CHAPTER 4

The Teachers' Perspectives and Their Implications

The attitudes, activities, and goals of classroom teachers are the most central determinants of the experiences of their students. Policymakers, superintendents, administrators, principals, and researchers can all express their views and exhort change, but if that call for change is not heard, accepted, and acted upon by classroom teachers, nothing changes at all. In the final stages of the Assessment for Learning and Progression (ALP) project in New Zealand, I interviewed a sample of teachers, individually and at length, from the 11 schools I had been working with. I asked the same questions of all the teachers, and audio-taped their responses, which left me free during the interview to follow things up and encourage further conversation about how the next steps they had suggested might be put into practice. I regarded the exercise as an opportunity for professional development as well as fact-finding. The teachers willingly gave 40–60 minutes of their non-teaching time to me, at a busy time of the year. Some of them said they enjoyed the opportunity to think and talk about important professional matters, and to be listened to intently. Such opportunities were rare, they said, and much appreciated.

I chose a cross section of teachers. The length of teaching experience within the sample ranged from five years to thirty. There were more women than men, especially from the elementary and middle/junior-high schools (called "intermediate schools" in New Zealand), but this reflects the gender balance within the schools as a whole. In the secondary schools, I focused on the English, math, and science departments, but included teachers from other departments who were suggested by their principals as particularly thoughtful, or who had a special responsibility for transition in a pastoral capacity.

All the students in the ALP project encountered transition most sharply when they moved to secondary schools (usually called "colleges" in New Zealand) at the end of what North Americans call grade 7. Some of these students had been in large elementary schools up to the end of grade 7. Others had been in two-year intermediate schools, catering to grade 6 and grade 7. Intermediate schools were created in New Zealand in the 1930s and are most common in urban areas. The students spend most of their time with one teacher at each grade level, although technology, music, and physical education are taught separately. Most intermediate teachers are trained initially as elementary-school teachers.

At the time of the study, there was minimal contact between the various stages of schooling in the Wellington region. Traditionally, elementary and intermediate teachers felt they had more in common with each other and less in common with the "colleges." They were also in separate and different unions, and, until 1997, they were paid at different rates, which tended to exacerbate the distrust between them, and may have been a further reason for the lack of communication between them.

These factors are all pertinent to what follows, but the particularities of the New Zealand system do not, I believe, mean that these teachers' views and concerns are unique to New Zealand and have no relevance elsewhere. You will need to decide for yourself whether they represent a reality you recognize. Each of the teachers in my sample is a fine professional, committed to students and education in his or her own ways, even if those ways are not identical. None of them occupies any moral high ground. The teachers may be puzzled by each other's practice, and sometimes by their own, but there is no doubting their shared desire to do the best job they can for the students they teach.

For the purposes of this chapter, I have divided the questions and the teachers' responses into two main sections. In the first section, I asked the teachers about their perceptions of how teaching in the "other" phase of education differs from what they themselves provide. I also asked where these perceptions originated. The second section deals with the teachers' thoughts about the barriers to learning at the time of transition from the elementary school to the secondary school. In the final stage of the interviews, I asked teachers for their views and suggestions about how these barriers might be reduced – if not removed. Their suggestions, along with many others, are offered in the final chapters.

Teachers' Perceptions About the "Other" Phase of Education

Here are some direct quotations from interviews with secondary-school teachers. (They often referred to the students as "kids," which is common practice in New Zealand and does not denote any lack of respect or affection.)

Secondary and intermediate schools are different branches of the same firm....We need to get over the old jealousies and forge much closer links, and with the elementary schools, too. It will mean establishing trust first, and then the mechanisms. (school counsellor)

This is very prejudiced, I know, but I often feel that the "eyes" of the curriculum are picked out at intermediate school....Kids get the fun things but not the draggy old boring things that we have to do. Very few kids get a real grounding in language. (head of English)

Intermediates tend to do more touchy-feely types of learning – group work; think, pair, share; artistic presentation. Secondaries just don't have time. (head of science)

I tried to use Cuisenaire rods with grade 9 students, and they said, "We don't want these, this is baby stuff." Playing is an important part of learning: students' concrete operational needs are often not met in secondary schools. (head of math)

Editing and proof-reading in elementary and intermediate seem to be about making the work neater rather than better. (head of English)

Intermediate kids are busy, doing set work, but there's no encouragement to go outside the parameters of the teacher and the task....That may be because of the insecurity of the teacher. (head of math)

Because I have a certain ability in math, I find it hard to imagine teachers who aren't confident with math. (math teacher)

Generally, in science they've done all the cool stuff and neglected the theory. (head of science)

It looks like elementary teachers are keen on telling the kids what they can do and not honest enough about the weaknesses. (head of science)

It's much harder to establish classroom routines when the kids see five or six people in a single day. (head of science)

I do feel for the kids and what they face when they leave intermediate, but we feel helpless in the face of all the things we're supposed to be doing and chasing the Holy Grail of national exams. (head of English)

We pretend that we will instantly know these kids better than their previous teachers, which is rubbish. (head of math)

Educators for grade 7 students in elementary/intermediate schools had this to say:

I have the impression that what elementary teachers do and think are vastly different from what happens at secondary. Elementary teachers try to teach, secondary just present. (teacher)

Elementary-trained teachers just seem intuitively to know what to do with kids – how to talk to them, use groups, use a variety of resources and so on – maybe because they've never had to teach to tests. (deputy principal)

Secondary-school teachers confuse poor literacy skills with poor capability. They underestimate the potential of the students. (teacher, whose early career was in secondary)

It's not surprising secondary school is subject-oriented – the secondary teachers haven't had a chance to learn about how to be teachers.... (teacher)

Maybe kids connect subject teaching with "growing up." (teacher)

I would feel guilty saying to a kid going to secondary who wasn't reading well, "Don't worry, your teachers will always have something for you to do" – because I'm not sure that they will. (language coordinator)

Secondary teachers deny responsibility for kids' learning beyond their own specialism – like when the kids can't read the resources in science, the science teachers say that's the English department's responsibility. (teacher)

The kids have a certain identity here, but over there it's just like cattle, constantly moving on. (teacher)

Kids in intermediate school have teachers who encourage and motivate them – all of a sudden that's gone. (science coordinator; science graduate, secondary trained)

It was mostly, "Come in, sit down, here's some notes, practise a few questions, do some problems, here's the homework, see you later." (teacher, commenting on his observations of math teaching in a local secondary school)

Why don't they let the kids make things in secondary school? Maybe they don't have the resources....probably the 50-minute teaching period makes a difference. (same teacher as above)

I can't envisage secondary kids working in groups. (teacher)

What does my impression of a secondary classroom look like? A couple of posters on the wall if you're lucky, and all the desks in rows. (teacher; consistently critical of secondary-school teaching methods)

The secondary teachers say, "It's different for you," but how different can it be? (teacher, after a visit from a secondary teacher to her classroom)

If we had a more positive mind-set about kids going on to college [secondary school] we might do more to prepare them.... it's hard because we don't know enough and we're a bit skeptical. (professional development coordinator)

If these comments leave you with an impression of a gulf in mutual understanding between secondary- and elementary-school teachers – often in schools located just a few metres apart – you would be right. For some years, there had been virtually no direct dealings between them. The ALP project had involved more shared encounters, and some shared activity, but many of the teachers were still unsure of what happened elsewhere and puzzled by what they were discovering. To fill out the picture in their minds, they drew from memories of their own school days, even 20 or 30 years before. Critical mutual stereotyping was the norm, good information was rare, and a non-judgmental acceptance of difference was even rarer. Blame was in the air, even while the need for closer liaison was being articulated.

As part of my analysis of the interviews, I looked for the frequency with which certain responses to some of the questions were mentioned. On the question of the origins of teachers' perceptions about the "other" phase, around 50 percent of the elementary teachers mentioned that their perceptions came from their own experiences at school; they acknowledged that their views were, therefore, probably outdated and coloured by some strong and often negative memories. For the secondary-school teachers, their perceptions came mainly from "contact with elementary teachers" (mentioned by 70 percent of the respondents), but not from seeing them teach. Only three of the sixteen secondary-school teachers interviewed had been in a working elementary classroom in the previous year or two. Only one of twenty-one elementary-school teachers had recent experience inside a working secondary classroom. For both groups, those who had children of their own at school had been influenced, understandably, by the experiences of their own children.

In one large secondary school, two key people – the guidance team leader, responsible for liaison with neighbouring elementary schools, and the head of the English department – had worked at the school for a combined total of nearly 50 years, and neither could remember visiting a working elementary classroom within the past 20 years. One had been aiming to do so for six months (since we first discussed it), but other more pressing issues (usually concerning continuing changes in the senior exams) had constantly taken priority.

Teachers' Views About "Barriers to Learning" at Transition

I needed to establish whether the teachers believed transition created barriers to learning for a significant proportion of the students, not just the odd one or two. Out of the 37 teachers in total, only three felt that there was not really a problem, and all three came from the same pair of schools. The secondary and elementary schools in this case were only a few metres apart, and the great majority of the elementary-school students went straight "next door" to continue their education. The social disruption involved in these circumstances was considerably less than in other schools with more confused patterns of transition.

For the remaining 34 teachers, transition from elementary school to secondary school did present barriers to the students, although there was no unanimity about the nature of these barriers. Seventy-five percent of the secondary teachers said that the main problem was that the students were "socially overwhelmed" in the new environment. This factor was mentioned by only 25 percent of the elementary teachers, who more commonly ascribed the problem to secondary-school teaching methods, puberty, the loss of security, and/or peer pressure to be "cool." When asked about which students they would expect to thrive or to struggle in the receiving school, about half the elementary teachers mentioned contact with home, or the decline in this contact, as a factor in transition, compared with only four of the secondary teachers who thought this.

The range of factors mentioned by secondary teachers as potential barriers at transition was huge – a total of 38 factors were identified. Those that were mentioned five or more times included the following:

- The more rigid structures and formal climate of the secondary school (8)
- Some new students being disruptive and demanding attention (5)
- Puberty and being "cool" with new peers, especially among boys (8)
- The overriding need to "fit in" with peers (5)
- Changes in teaching and learning strategies (8)
- Learning not respected at home, and parents "give up" (6)
- Secondary-school teachers see too many students, and lose the personal contact the students have been used to (although this can return in the senior years) of secondary school (6)

Some of the most telling and illuminating analysis of the difficulties faced by students and their teachers in the first year at secondary school came from the teachers themselves:

> *Somewhere in grade 8 you see the bright-eyed student change into the person who just looks at you and shrugs.*

In some of our schools, "It's cool to be a fool." Some of our kids get rotten role models from the older students.

The student who asks a lot of questions is more likely to succeed, but the formality of the new school inhibits them.

For some kids, the change to secondary school is an organizational nightmare.

For some of our Samoan students, being part of the group is more important than individual achievement.

When they come and see round the school, we give them a "magic show" in the science labs, but that's not what real science is about. We start them off with boiling water and more mundane stuff.

Some kids have multiple minor clashes with different teachers throughout the day, and these gradually turn into major trouble.

By the time we've got a good picture of the grade 8s as learners, the year is halfway through.

The pace of change for senior secondary requirements is so fast that you end up "punch-drunk," and this pushes the junior years lower down the list of priorities. If we could really focus on grades 8 and 9, it would make the later years much easier for us.

It doesn't sound good when you say it out loud, but maybe we know they'll be okay by the end of grade 8, because they spend most of the year repeating things they've done before.

The elementary-school teachers mentioned, five or more times, the following potential barriers to learning out of a total of 27 factors mentioned:

- Changing teaching strategies (7)
- Declining rapport with teachers (6)
- Puberty and the social distraction from learning (8)
- Fragmentation of teaching into subjects (5)
- Sheer size of the receiving school (5)
- Loss of sense of security and of being "looked after" (5)

For this group, comments about difficulties in the first year of secondary school were more circumspect as they were further away from the actual experience. Some of their comments reflect their own management of students new to the intermediate school and how that must correspond to the secondary transition.

> *If you're given stuff to read every lesson that you just can't manage, your self-esteem just collapses.*

> *One of my kids came back to see me after a week at the high school and said, "I've had five detentions already because I keep asking what to do."*

> *I teach the same kids every day, and even for me it can take most of the first term to re-establish a good learning environment to the point where you can really teach rather than just manage behaviour. When you only see the kids for a few periods a week, that must take even longer.*

> *Some kids still need "morning talks," even just once a week, to let the social stuff out before you start working.*

> *By this age, the kids are far more concerned about friends than about academic things. It's hard for them to break away from their friends if they need to.*

> *If secondary teachers can't reach down to where the kids are at, the kids are failing before they start.*

> *The social side of school can be a battering experience and self-esteem is so important....*

Teachers' Views About Information Passed From Elementary School to Secondary School

During the ALP project, we spent hours on this issue, exploring the advantages and disadvantages of various strategies. Sometimes, it felt as if the details would never be resolved until and unless the teachers understood and trusted one another more. Once such trust is established, really difficult issues start to look so much easier. Below are the questions and some of the responses about the organization of information about the students at transition.

Question: What kind of information should be passed on?
The following information should be passed on:

- What the student has been taught
- What the student has learned and can do
- Academic skills, knowledge, and understanding, usually identified within subjects or areas of learning
- More generic learning skills and work habits
- Personal and social characteristics
- Family background and circumstances
- Special learning needs
- Friendship groups, and which students need to be separated for their own good
- Health problems and needs
- Overall ability, relative to other students in the cohort

Some of these items are relatively non-contentious: everyone accepts that the receiving school needs to know a student's date of birth, address, health needs, where and how to contact the family in an emergency, and the name of the providing school. Such information is factual and essential to the school's duty of care. Beyond these essentials, teachers' views begin to diverge. More teachers in elementary schools than secondary teachers were interested in the individual student's strengths, talents, and potential. Subject-related "competence" information was wanted by 75 percent of the secondary teachers, whereas only 50 percent of the elementary teachers regarded this as a priority. On the question of reading competence, 60 percent of the secondary teachers wanted it, and only 30 percent of elementary teachers had it high on their list. Only 15 percent of secondary teachers were interested in a statement about the student's personality, with a similar number feeling strongly that this would be too subjective and that the student should be allowed a fresh start in the new environment.

Surrounding all these possibilities was a sense of frustration about the time it takes to write down all the information on each student, about the plethora of different demands made by different secondary schools, and about the inconsistencies among different elementary schools in completing the information. At a deeper layer again was the suspicion in elementary schools that the next teacher would be unwilling to read what the previous teacher has said, and probably would be unable to use the information anyway because of the dominance of "curriculum coverage" over "real" teaching.

Question: How much information is needed, and how should it be arranged?

All the teachers agreed that information should be concise and manageable to both write and read, but when they began to talk in detail the problem was keeping it sufficiently concise. Making information look less by cramming everything onto a single sheet of paper was not helpful, as different pieces of information would be needed by different groups at the receiving school. Some school principals and the people most interested in IT applications could see great potential in communicating electronically between schools. At first glance, the possibilities were attractive, but for a number of reasons I encouraged the schools to mark time for a while, to let the quality, validity, and reliability of the information available catch up with the electronic potential. Although it might look more impressive, poor information in electronic form is still poor information.

As a first step, teachers would have to agree on the nature of the information to be gathered and communicated, taking account of manageability for both teams of teachers, as well as doing justice to the students. Second, coded judgments based on perceptions of achievement against certain criteria would have to be checked for consistency both in and among the schools using these codes. Without such checks, the information might appear to be reliable, but, in reality, would not be. Third, teachers would need access to the right hardware and software, or generating the information might end up more time-consuming than writing it. Fourth, we should never lose sight of the idiosyncrasies and uniqueness of individual students by reducing them to data that suit the mechanisms of the software. Examples of a student's work, if needed, could be scanned into his or her own file. Students could create their own additions to their files in the form of a

> **Pause & Reflect**
>
> Given the technological confidence and the competence of today's students, should we encourage them – as part of their transition – to gather "digital portfolios" representing their learning that they can show to their next teacher? What are the logistical implications of this idea?

"letter to the next school." The more sophisticated school IT systems could handle all of this, but the low-tech alternative of paper and pen is still available.

Question: Why is information for progression always tricky?

No matter how sophisticated the technology available to us, the essentials are quite simple. Relevant, agreed-upon information about students needs to be identified, communicated, manageable, and then used to assist students' learning in the receiving environment. Potential barriers to this endeavour are the same now as they have always been, and always will be. Many years ago, when computerized records were merely a twinkle in someone's eye, I drew up a list of potential barriers to effective transfer of information, and the same list still applies to the most sophisticated of systems today:

- Information about previous learning is not available, or not available in time to be useful to the receivers
- Information about previous learning is available, but does not include what the receivers really want to know
- Information about previous learning is available, but is not considered to be trustworthy by the receiving teachers
- School systems, the numbers of incoming students, and the number of providing schools all overwhelm the ability to see each incoming student as an individual with unique needs
- Receiving teachers are either unwilling or unable to amend their teaching plans to take account of information about previous learning

Providing and receiving teachers do not understand enough about the next and the previous classroom or school to make sense of the information that passes between them. To some degree, the above difficulties exist whenever students move from one teacher or school to the next. At the point of transfer from elementary to secondary, these problems are merely exacerbated by a number of other factors.

Question: How can students become involved in information transfer?

The teachers in the ALP project were not asked directly about the possibilities of involving the students in presenting themselves to their receiving school and new teachers. This issue has been dominated by administrative and bureaucratic considerations in the past, and, therefore, is outside the realm of the students.

The suggestion that each student writes a letter to his or her new teachers, as part of the information to be brought to the receiving school seems, at first, to be an answer to a number of questions. It would illuminate the uniqueness of the student without asking teachers to write at length on behalf of the student. It would encourage students to think seriously about moving to the next school and the goals they want to pursue there. It would be a pleasing symbol of the centrality of the student, a refreshing alternative to the complexities of teacher judgments, form filling, and computerization.

Beyond the initial idea, it was the detail – as ever – that made the teachers think more deeply about exactly what would happen, and what the implications might be. We had to start with clarity about the purpose and audience of a student letter, just as we ask about purpose and audience every time a record or report is under review. In this case, we ran into a problem straight away. Some secondary teachers were interested in seeing a sample of the student's unaided writing. They believed a student's writing capability was a major factor for success (or failure) in many secondary classrooms. A letter was a neat solution to their need to learn something about the student as a person and have a preview of the student's writing at the same time.

We only had to look at this suggestion from the point of view of the student to see the flaw. If I were the student, I would want to present myself positively to my receiving school, in a way that made others see me as a real person, not just as a "writer," especially if I knew that my writing could be criticized as untidy or inaccurate. How I write, the "medium," could distract from the "message" about me.

These two potential purposes of the student letter need to be dealt with separately. By all means, as part of the picture-of-learning capability that the next teachers have to plan for, offer a sample of each student's unaided handwriting to the receiving school. But let the students decide how they want to present themselves, so that the medium and the message support rather than work against each other. Alternatively, have students keep their letters to show to their new teachers when they first encounter them. Some students may be uncomfortable communicating in public among peers they do not yet know and trust. These students may prefer to communicate with their new teachers privately.

Of course, these ideas are not new for many schools. They follow logically from the idea of a "record or portfolio of achievement," which contains items that indicate a student's development. These items have been selected and deselected through a process of periodic review by the students during their time at school. Such a process can start in the early years of schooling, and continue right through to the end. When the process and the product are both working well, the record/portfolio can be a central component of the information that accompanies the student from school to school.

With so many complex issues, there are no simple solutions to the question of involving the students in their transition. Each school is unique. You cannot just leapfrog into a new system without laying some foundations. Students need help and some practice in thinking about their learning and personal strengths, their needs, and their goals before they are confident enough to present themselves well. Parents, too, need to be properly informed about what the receiving school is proposing, and reassured about its purpose. Finally, receiving teachers need to think about how they can use the information offered by the students, both constructively and respectfully.

Question: What is the best timing for information transfer?
The ALP project teachers could provide no absolute solutions to the problem of timing for the transfer of information from school to school. They recognized that the long summer break from school has such an impact on some students' learning that good information gathered late in the school year seems inaccurate while students adjust to the new school. All students need a period of adjustment and time to settle down.

Those in receiving schools who arrange the groupings and schedules of the incoming students sometimes want information far too early. In some cases, six months or more might elapse between information being requested by the secondary school and the arrival of students to the receiving school. When this happens, the bureaucratic needs of the "system" can leave teachers in the providing school with the impression that their students are not expected to make real progress during their last six months. This is a veiled insult to both them and their students.

However strong the need for simplicity, student information needs to be gathered and used in two main stages, depending on the purpose of the information. For administrative/bureaucratic purposes, some information will be needed in the last few weeks of the year in the providing school. Once the information is in the receiving school, secondary-school teachers may not be ready to look at it until the end of the old school year or just before the start of the new school year. Even if the receiving teachers are unable to absorb all the details of their new students' learning capabilities, they can show an interest in what their students have learned before. By using an open-ended approach to tasks during the first week, teachers can determine students' needs by observing their approach to learning in the new classroom.

One secondary-school math-department head talked about the timing of information for the department, and for herself as a classroom teacher. For the department, she liked having access to some of the data about the incoming students' grades in the various math strands (for example, number, problem-solving, geometry) toward the end of the school year. This gave her and her colleagues the chance to look at the patterns and trends for the new students, to review their resources, to amend some of the time frames in the first few weeks of the program, and to take note of particular students and their needs at both ends of the capability spectrum. It became part of the end-of-year review and goal setting for the department.

As a classroom teacher, she explained that her needs and the timing were slightly different. She could look at individual student's records before she met the student, but the information would not stick, because it was decontextualized – she could not connect it to a particular student. Although she scanned the records for patterns and trends, she put them aside for the first few teaching periods. She preferred to use some fairly open-ended diagnostic activities to get a feel for her students as a group and as individuals. These activities allowed her to watch the students at work, listen to them talk about math, and recognize the different circumstances the students were dealing with. After a few weeks, when she was able to connect the name and face of each student, she was ready to compare her early impressions with the information sent by the previous teacher. From the records, she was able to take note of all sorts of information she might have ignored before she met her students.

Prevailing Myths

Before turning to the final two chapters of this book, let me take a moment to reflect on two myths most commonly encountered when the conversation turns to elementary-school/secondary-school relationships. Both myths have affected our respect for the other for decades. It is time to debunk them.

Myth 1: Elementary-school teachers teach students; secondary teachers teach subjects.

This myth is often cited as the difference between elementary and secondary approaches to teaching. As a secondary-school teacher, I was always unhappy with this generalization. Earlier in this book, I urged us to accept the complexity of the elementary/secondary transition, and I think the time has come to get past this oversimplification. Yes, elementary-school teachers are in continual contact with a group of students for a year or more and become acutely aware of the uniqueness of each student. Their role as the student's only or main teacher allows them to work through and beyond subject divisions. They may well have been attracted to teaching in the first place by a passion for students rather than a passion for any one aspect of learning.

Many secondary-school teachers, too, are keenly interested in their students as young people, rather than as mere recipients of the teacher's enthusiasm for a subject. They, too, may have wanted to teach for a host of reasons, and their specialist subject is the context for a wider interest in teaching, not an end in itself. The continual stereotyping of secondary teachers as "subject specialists," with all the negative connotations attached to that, is unhelpful to all, as well as being unfair to some. Similarly, the secondary-school stereotype of every elementary-school teacher as a "low-order generalist" with no interest in specialist subject matter is inaccurate, unhelpful, and unfair. It is all part of the blaming culture that we need to move beyond.

Myth 2: Teachers in every receiving school want students to make a "fresh start."

Logistical complexity bedevils the passing on of information about students to such a degree that sometimes the idea of a fresh start looks terribly tempting. Very occasionally, teachers say that a fresh start is the best choice for their students. Much more often, though, we need to distinguish between a fresh start in behaviour, which may be helpful, and a fresh start in learning, which is not helpful. Even if a student has not encountered a subject before, no learner is ever a blank slate to be written on. The vast majority of teachers I encounter are clearly aware of that, even if the implications are hard to handle.

Most principals and other school leaders know this, too. But in these competitive times, there are pressures to present one's school as completely different from what has happened before or elsewhere. These pressures can be hard to resist. There is overwhelming evidence about the need to sustain the confidence and self-efficacy of learners. This need cannot be served by criticizing or denying all previous learning. Parents, too, have to feel confident that learning improvement is both possible and expected, without losing faith in what has gone before.

Is It Just "Too Hard"?

If the successful management of learning progression from elementary school to secondary school was easy, we would have solved it by now. Getting it right is much more complicated than we may want to admit. It goes way beyond information gathering and into some of the most fundamental and intractable questions that face us as a profession. The following are some questions to think about in increasingly competitive environments:

- How do we foster a collaborative and positive climate among all the schools serving a community?
- How do we balance the organizational needs of schools and the uniqueness of each student?
- How do we support secondary teachers, who have to meet the individual learning needs of more than 100 students?
- How do we support an elementary teacher, who has to be confident and skilled in the full range of "subjects"?

- How can we monitor the overall learning of secondary-school students when their teachers never get the chance to talk to each other?

Of course, it helps to be aware of the need to persevere, and to take a multidimensional look at the transition problem. To this end, in the final chapters of this book I return to the "five bridges" identified by the Cambridge research team in their 1999 study. Taking these five categories of strategies, we will gather a wide range of experiences and ideas. None of these can be seen in isolation. It is not a how-to checklist. It is a way of stimulating the customized planning required in schools, both individually and as partners in a wider family of schools, caring together for every community's students and young people.

Pause & Reflect

What kinds of information would you find most useful when you encounter a group of students for the first time? What are the practical issues surrounding the gathering and passing on of this information, and how might these issues be resolved?

CHAPTER 5

Building the Bridges of Progression

As you will recall from chapter 2, each of the five bridges below describes a category of strategies designed to enhance and support learners as they move from one school to the next. This ensures that the progress they have made continues and their learning moves forward with them. The five bridges are:

1. The managerial/bureaucratic bridge
2. The social/personal bridge
3. The curriculum-content bridge
4. The pedagogical bridge
5. The learning-to-learn bridge

The Cambridge researchers found that the first three bridges are easier to manage than the last two; however, the last two bridges have the most positive influence on the quality of students' continued learning. Other research about the impact of assessment on learning shows the powerful effects of assessment for feedback and the importance of involving the students as active partners in the review of their own learning and in setting their own goals.

Before discussing each bridge, we need to state and understand one basic premise. All of these strategies need the foundation of a particular attitude of mind – everyone involved must genuinely believe in the potential for learning and achievement of the students they share. They must accept shared responsibility, along with families and the students themselves, for developing this potential. They must avoid blame, and try to leave the baggage of the past behind. All this is harder to do than it sounds, as it may mean a change of attitude, which is more difficult than starting from scratch. Given this foundation, what does experience tell us about the first bridge?

The Managerial/Bureaucratic Bridge

This first bridge involves two key strategies: (1) meetings and (2) organizing the transfer of information.

Meetings

Establish a pattern of regular, but not too frequent, meetings between the principals/administrators of the elementary and secondary schools in your community or district. The patterns of transition might be quite complicated. While the purpose of the group may not be to manage each student's progression from elementary to secondary school, it is important everyone involved in the transition keep in touch. This can be done primarily by email or by letter, but a periodic meeting is a good way to build trust and provide the clarity that is needed in the early stages of a good relationship.

Where the group meets seems to matter. Why not move the meetings from school to school? This gives all participants the opportunity to welcome guests to their school, have a look around, talk to people, and watch students at work. If the group lacks leadership, and a "neutral" person is not available to help, move the chairing of the group around, or agree for someone to take on the role of chair for a year at a time. Everyone at the meeting will have pressing demands on their time, so make sure to have prompt starting and finishing times, a clear focus and purpose of the meeting, and a brief written record of the outcomes.

It should be completely unnecessary to remind anyone about the protocols of an effective meeting – about listening, being respectful, keeping to agreed-upon items under discussion. Here again, when involved with people with whom you do not normally work, be especially careful about your assumptions. Different schools and teams have different ways of doing things. It may even be useful to clarify some basic ground rules or protocols whenever a new group is established.

When principals get together in a group for the first time, they are understandably very aware of one another. One of the unintended slights that can occur is the decision by one member to be represented at the meetings by his or her vice-principal. There may be good rational reasons for this substitution. For example, the vice-principal may be responsible for the student transitions, the principal might have other (more important) matters to attend to, or the principal may feel that he or she has been out of the school too much lately. Nonetheless, the decision to not attend carries quite a message to the other group members, especially in the early stages of the group's development – before mutual trust has been established. The message may be interpreted as, "You feel you're more important than the rest of us," or, "This issue is a marginal one for you."

In each of the schools represented in this group, the inference of the principal's involvement is clearly seen by the rest of the staff. Teachers will take their cue from what they see, and the habit of constructive liaison with other schools can grow from there, encouraged with practical strategies as well as symbolic ones. Here are some suggestions:

- The administrative links between and among schools can oil the wheels of other strategies for putting teachers in touch with one another. Teachers who visit classrooms and teachers in a different school provide rich professional development, and need to be guided and funded, rather than leaving such encounters entirely to chance and informal connections.

- The professional development coordinators/consultants of a family of schools can spend some very useful time together, identifying the range of expertise that teachers can draw upon. Mentoring, pairings of individuals or teams of teachers, teachers' professional book groups, shared action research – all of these need some administrative help to get them going and to keep them going.

- Put together an agreed-upon transition record or portfolio, or improve on the systems already in place. This is harder to do than it sounds. However, once a reasonably trusting, no-blame climate is established, a group representing the schools can try to juggle the various and sometimes conflicting needs of the parties involved. Discussion among each school's representative can help to build the empathy required for effective liaison, and the exercise is satisfyingly concrete for those who appreciate tangible outcomes.

- Plan and manage a shared Professional Day across a family of schools that serves different age ranges. To do this well takes many hours of shared planning that starts months ahead of time. For the professional day to be considered a success, teachers need to feel that they have gained and learned something useful and are willing to continue the connection. A well-organized and successful shared day can be the springboard for further collaboration. If a significant number of teachers, for whatever reasons, consider the day a waste of their time, they may be discouraged from spending further professional time together. Teachers' time is a very precious commodity: one shared day for a family of schools can involve hundreds of teacher hours.

Organizing the Transfer of Information

As we have seen in chapter 4, it may take a group of schools a while to decide on how best to achieve the most effective and efficient procedures. The leaders of the various schools involved may delegate the decisions on the details to those most involved in providing and using information in their schools. That does not mean that the delegated task then drops below the principal's horizon. Consistent interest and encouragement are needed from principals to ensure that the process is successfully designed and then implemented. The business of information transfer comes clearly within the parameters of the managerial strategies identified as "the managerial/bureaucratic bridge."

The Social/Personal Bridge

In the last few years, many schools have improved their strategies for building this bridge. We are improving in our goal to ease students socially into their new environment. It is important to listen to students when they tell us about their fears of getting lost, of being bullied, and of being overwhelmed by the anti-learning culture that many young people impute to their older peers and the "culture of cool."

Before the Transfer

Many opportunities to build social bridges occur before the student transfers to the "big school," at whatever age. Here are six of the most effective and useful opportunities to consider:

1. Senior elementary students, in the year or two before they transfer, can visit the local secondary school for some specialist teaching, or to use specialist resources that they would not have access to otherwise. These visits allow them to see the school at work, to begin to find their way around, to check out the locations of the

washrooms, to see some familiar faces among students who left their school the year before, and to meet some of the teaching and support staff. An even more impressive strategy for establishing positive role models in the minds of the younger students is to encourage secondary-school students to work alongside the younger ones, coaching them how to use specialist equipment, for example, or explaining a skill area they may not have encountered before. These senior students may have attended the same elementary school, take the same bus to school, or live on the same street. Many of these older students may have been feared by the younger students, and now they are demonstrating some of the interesting activities the secondary school has to offer. Reducing soon-to-be transition students' anxieties about working in a new environment need not be a whole-year commitment. Most students will adapt quickly once they can see how the new environment works. It is the not knowing that worries them most.

2. There are many other opportunities for visiting the secondary school, beyond the rather dry "walk-about," which almost all schools organize for incoming students. If the schools are close enough together, after-school extra-curricular activities can be opened up to prospective students. This could be a privilege for elementary-school students in their final year, in recognition of the important step they are about to take. Offering students membership in a school band, drama group, or chess club might be especially helpful for incoming students who are less skilled socially or less confident academically. Some students revel in the larger social group that secondary school presents to them; for others, it is a nightmare until they find some like-minded peers.

3. Make visits from the secondary school to the elementary school part of the plan. For example, enable secondary-school staff, if they wish, to spend a small proportion of their time in the elementary-school environment, perhaps providing a specialist input that is not available otherwise. Teaching a second language is the most common focus of such a strategy. The secondary school is deliberately investing some of its resources – perhaps two teacher hours per week for each school involved, plus travel time – in the

long-term "engagement" of its prospective students. There will be students receiving this program who choose in the end to go to other schools, and that is okay. All students, at this burgeoning stage in their learning lives and before the major social upheaval happens, can benefit from a widening of their horizons, both personally and culturally. Staff at both the elementary and secondary schools also find the visits rewarding.

The development of such a plan must have the positive approval of the elementary schools involved. Further, participants from the secondary school must not regard the visits as "doing a favour" for a neighbouring school, but as a definite enhancement of the students' experience. While the benefits to the students are hard to quantify, they are easy to see. Students will know one more face when they arrive in their new environment. There will be someone in the receiving school who has seen the students in their learning environment.

The secondary school, too, benefits from a better understanding of its new students. The teachers who visit the "partner" schools work there and pick up the talk in the staff room. They are also in a position to offer information to teachers whose view of the secondary school may need updating. In this sense, the student-centred social/personal purpose of this strategy quickly merges into another very valuable link – the teachers.

4. Another purpose for pre-transfer visits from secondary-school teachers to elementary schools is to talk to parents. Traditionally, the secondary school's first meeting with parents takes place at the secondary school. It does not have to be this way. Elementary schools are happy to invite the parents of its older students, and the students themselves, to the school to meet the principal and other key people from local secondary schools. The familiar elementary-school surroundings are less daunting for some parents than the secondary school. Parents can see, firsthand, the respect and professionalism of those who currently manage their children's learning and of those who are about to. The "known" can mediate the introduction to the "unknown." Sometimes, older secondary-school students come, too, to talk from their perspective about their experiences.

5. Before families make their choice of secondary school, invite representatives of the local secondary schools to meet parents to explain how their schools manage the successful "induction" of incoming students. In one instance, some of the schools mistook the purpose of the meeting, and began with a preamble about the virtues of the school, the hockey team, the facilities, and so on. "No," said the parents patiently (this was a very affluent community), "we want to know how you are going to make our children feel at home in your school and ensure that their learning progresses/transitions smoothly." The schools had no choice but to respond, and very illuminating it was, too, to hear the assumptions that were made about incoming students' needs.

6. Another form of visiting from secondary to elementary school can involve the students. Some social-education programs in the elementary school may already have built-in suggestions: senior students are invited to talk to their younger peers about resisting the negative peer pressures that the young students themselves worry about. Older students can offer advice to their younger peers who will listen more readily to them than to advice from their teachers.

After the Transfer

Many opportunities to build social bridges also occur after the student transfers to the "big school," at whatever age. Here are three of the most effective and useful opportunities to consider:

1. After new students arrive at the secondary school, a variety of useful strategies can be used to settle them in. Older students can be trained as mentors and, in groups, individually, or in pairs, show new students around the school, help with administrative details, answer questions, and provide support and encouragement in any way they can. Some schools maintain this attachment for several weeks, or even for the whole first year, although by the end of the first term many younger students no longer need (or want) help. By then, what they may need is time to catch up on learning, which they may have ignored while they were distracted by the novelty of the receiving school.

2. Some secondary schools provide a special orientation program for new students during the first few days of the school year. Together,

these students work through the "Welcome to Your New School" booklet, which explains all the day-to-day things they need to know about – how the school works, who is who, and what is where. Occasionally, the orientation program may directly address the differences in teaching and learning that await them. In the United Kingdom (UK), some schools have a "learning-to-learn" program for incoming students that focuses on how students can develop their learning skills and improve their overall success in the receiving school.

3. Very occasionally, a secondary school focuses on identifying students' learning styles, asks about their prior learning, and looks at their records/profiles of achievement. Some students find this a little unnerving in the company of people they do not know well. They worry about being exposed or laughed at, and may not be as forthcoming as their teachers might wish. If the students are relatively relaxed, and a good group climate has been created, this early focus on learning can provide a necessary reminder that school is about working, as well as about meeting new people. We need to be honest with our students about what they will find hard, in addition to all the information about the "cool" stuff they will find in their new environment. Above all, students need evidence of high expectations, and they need encouragement that they can do it.

> **Pause & Reflect**
> What do the schools in your community do to ensure that students settle down socially when they move to the secondary school?

The Curriculum-Content Bridge

Continuity of content is one of the purposes that provincial/territorial and national curriculums are designed to fulfill. Logically, it makes sense for all the students passing through an education system to be taught certain things in common, which are arranged so that the content flows smoothly from one stage of education to the next. Unfortunately, in almost every case, the new curriculums are overstuffed, so loaded with detail and worries about compliance and coverage that schools are completely distracted from the essentials of good learning. One impact of this rapid change in teaching requirements is to make teachers focus on their own slice of the curriculum in isolation from the others. They lose sight of what the students were learning before they arrived, or after they moved on. In the secondary school, the priority for each department is to manage its own content – managing the overlap between subjects and departments is not a priority, to the long-term detriment of teachers' workload and students' learning. Liaison between schools actually declines in many cases, until the schools get their confidence back and begin to rebuild their relationships.

The dust cloud stirred up by the introduction of new curriculums seems to last about five years, or less if the principal is really clear and confident about how to manage the change process. When the dust clears a little, we can see beyond the confines of our own schools, and view the possible advantages of finding out what is going on around us. In secondary schools, departments find ways of sharing their plans and expectations for cohorts of students, ensuring that connections are made if they are useful and students are able to make sense of what they are learning as a whole. This is about building curriculum-content bridges across different parts of the same school. In elementary schools, shared planning can make a positive difference to the quality of teaching and the spread of best practices.

Sharing Curriculum Content

To ensure smooth continuity of learning between elementary and secondary schools, here are four suggestions:

1. The simplest strategy is for elementary and secondary schools to exchange copies of the work overview or teaching plans being used in the grade levels immediately before and after the transition. No extra work is involved – these plans should already exist. For example, for teachers in the elementary school, this means sending a copy of the relevant parts of the math program to the math departments in the secondary schools that most of their students plan to attend. In return, the elementary-school math coordinator asks for a copy of the math program that students are following in their first year at those secondary schools.

    When there is a degree of trust between the schools, and when the key people have actually met, these plans will be looked at with interest. Questions and concerns will arise quite quickly: teachers may discover unplanned repetition of key activities and need to talk about how this can be turned into planned consolidation. If the plans include examples of tests or other assessment strategies, teachers might want to compare their expectations. Student exemplars of expected standards are also very useful for spotting where the discontinuities might creep in.

Once the plans on paper have been looked at and the questions identified, then it may be time for the math coordinators from the elementary schools to meet with the secondary-school math department heads. At the end of this chapter, I suggest an activity for such a meeting that focuses on the practicalities of task design, managing learning, making sound judgments, developing next steps, and so on.

2. It may be possible for groups of interested teachers from the different schools to plan a shared task together. This task can then be given to all the students they teach at a specified time. Afterwards, the teachers can reconvene to talk about how the students fared. Here again, the climate among the teachers will have to allow for this to happen without judgment, defensiveness, and blame. Teachers will uncover differences of perception and interpretation – something to be expected and a necessary first step toward improving relations between schools. If the time frames for change are reasonable, the job is worth doing, and the workload can be tackled in relatively easy stages, then teachers will feel they can sustain the motivation needed to help students with the transition.

3. Much has been written over the years about "bridging units" – topics or projects that are started in one school and continued in the next. The idea is attractive in some respects. For a start, it requires teachers from different schools to work together, pooling ideas, experiences, and resources. This may actually be the most professionally productive part of the exercise, a case where process is more useful than product. For the students, the message of continuity is a very powerful one, especially if the teachers can cross over during the course of the unit, with some secondary-school teachers contributing in the elementary school and vice versa.

The logistics of bridging units can cause problems when the secondary school draws from schools whose students have not been involved in the pre-transfer parts of the unit. In urban areas, where students can bypass the local school to attend one on the other side of town, there are few clear patterns of movement from elementary school to secondary school. In the first year of secondary school, then, some students would have started the bridging unit and others would not have. Those from schools not involved in the bridging unit could feel excluded, though through no fault of their own. This can create quite a challenge for the teacher. "It's not fair," might be heard almost immediately from these students unless the teacher knows how to handle the situation. To overcome such a problem, each "half" of the unit could be designed to "stand alone," or a review process could be included to give students who had missed the first half the opportunity to catch up.

> **Pause & Reflect**
> Would all students welcome carrying on with a topic they had started in the previous school?

Here is one final thought about bridging units, from the students' perspective. The students in the New Zealand research study said almost unanimously that they wanted their next teachers to know about and build on their previous learning. This does not mean they wanted to cover the same things.

Entry into secondary school is perceived by most students to be a "rite of passage." These students are excited by the move to secondary school, because it is different, and they expect to be treated more like grown-ups. For them, the continuity that the bridging unit is designed to provide may be a source of irritation. For others, however, the move to secondary school can be intimidating, and the differences are too much. For these students, the continuity of a bridging unit may be helpful. The purpose of a bridging unit is to motivate and engage the students: if it fails to do so because of students' reactions to it, we might be better advised to focus on the continuity of teaching methods, not curriculum content.

4. Share standards, to achieve a greater understanding of the shared curriculum. In my work with teachers in various countries over the past few years, I have been trying to improve teachers' understanding of each other across the structures of schooling that threaten to

divide them. In the UK and New Zealand, expected outcomes are described in terms of "levels," and eight or nine levels are used for the full spectrum of learning from age 5 to around age 16. In Canada, "levels" are defined within a year/grade rather than across a band of years. There are advantages and disadvantages for each approach. One advantage of the "level" approach is that it encourages teachers from different year levels to talk to each other about what they think these "levels" actually mean, and what they look like in samples of students' work. This is necessary to improve the reliability (consistency and fairness) of the judgments made by teachers and reported to parents and to the next teacher. Until quite recently, "levels" in Canada have been about the range of standards within a grade level, but current development of "performance standards" is enabling teachers to see the progression in skills from one grade to the next.

What does all this have to do with a better understanding between the teachers of different age groups? Below is an activity for teachers that I – and many others – began using several years ago in the UK as a means of standardizing (that is, making more reliable) teachers' judgments of their students' levels of attainment within the framework of the required curriculum.

At first, we focused on sharing standards among teachers of the same year group, or chronological bands of two or three years. When I realized the activity was a useful professional-development exercise, I started to use it with teachers on both sides of the transition between elementary and secondary schools. The rationale behind this was twofold. First, it improved the common understanding and use of a level as a shorthand way of describing a student's achievement. Second, and more important, it provided a structure for more fundamental conversations about the tasks we set for students, how we support their learning, how we analyze and derive meaning from what they do, and how we use this to establish worthwhile next steps in learning for them.

Something to Try

Here is an activity to try: Bring together a group of teachers from two or three different grade levels and, preferably, from the years on either side of the elementary to secondary transition. You will need to agree to meet four or five times, for about one hour on each occasion if you are meeting after school. A much better option, if possible, is to meet twice, for two or three hours each time, at the beginning of the day rather than at the end. These meetings can be quite demanding and work much better when people are not tired after a full day of teaching.

You may need a neutral facilitator who understands what the group is trying to achieve – someone who can focus all of his or her attention on guiding the group through its discussions.

As a group, choose an element of the curriculum that you want to focus on. Most people start with some form of writing, which is easier than starting with something less tangible and familiar. Next, design a task that you will use to illuminate the students' standard or level of achievement, using the criteria described in the curriculum. You will need to decide whether the assessment task can be used as a freestanding piece or be part of a teaching module. The task needs to be open-ended enough to be tackled with some success by all your students. Alternatively, have only one age level of students attempt the task, and have teachers at the other age levels help judge the outcomes, even though their own students have not been directly involved. There are advantages and disadvantages to each way of doing this; you choose.

This shared task helps the discussion later about what the students have done, because everyone understands what the task is about. If you wish, ask everyone in the group to bring in samples of writing done by students in the normal course of their class work. If you do that, be prepared for some potentially tedious explanations of different tasks before you discuss the outcomes.

Have teachers whose students are involved in this activity pick one or two examples of what they think achievement looks like at the top of the range, at the bottom, and in the middle.

To make the group's discussion of these samples manageable, ask someone to make a preliminary selection of the samples that will spark good conversation and that will be easier to reproduce. If your focus is writing, it is a good idea to pick some samples in which a student's handwriting and presentation belie the actual quality of the content – that is, a good piece of writing, but poor handwriting, and vice versa. This exercise helps teachers realize the need to get past some of the cosmetics of students' writing, which can be a distraction. This is not to dismiss the cosmetics of writing, but to show that writing assessment includes other things – the structure of the writing, "voice," its impact on the reader, and so on.

(cont'd. on next page)

You may want to make the work samples into overhead transparencies or slides or put them on an interactive whiteboard for everyone to see, but I find that most teachers still prefer to have the samples in their hands so that they can make notes on them if they wish.

Before you start looking at the samples, go back to the criteria for the levels you are looking for, and review what you think these criteria actually mean. What are the key words in the level criteria? How do these levels differ from each other? Do not get too bogged down doing this exercise. The shared meaning will probably only emerge as you look together at what the criteria look like, not when you decontextualize the words themselves. Some teachers have a tendency to get very picky about the meanings of words, which can drive other people crazy, especially at the end of the day. The group chair or facilitator can decide when it is time to stop looking at words and start looking at the work itself. You could go straight to the samples, of course, but I have found it helps to clarify a few key words first, to avoid having to stop and start all the time.

When you start to look at the work samples, be prepared to look at each one really carefully. To add structure to your discussion, use the annotation form (see figure 5.1), and complete the questions as you go along.

If you decide to become involved in the above-mentioned activity, several kinds of things will crop up as you do so. Some of these are discussed below.

Identifying the Student

It is not necessary to identify the students. Age and grade level can also be omitted. These omissions are deliberate for two reasons. First, you are not talking about the students but about their work. It is too easy to start explaining the work in terms of a student's history, family, and social behaviour, which can distract from the focus on what the student has actually done. Second, you may want to use some of the samples as examples of what is or is not required for specific levels or standards. When these work samples are shown to someone else – another teacher, parents, or other students – it is important to protect the identities of the works' creators.

Context

Here are some questions to ask.

Question: What was the student asked to do?

If you have used an agreed-upon task, the answer to this question is easy. If not, the teacher whose work sample is being looked at will explain the

Annotation Sheet for a Sample of Student Work

Age of student in years and months (if known)

Grade

Context/Task

1. What was the student asked to do?

2. How much support was provided if any?

3. Which are the main learning expectations/outcomes in this task?

Analysis

1. Which characteristics of this work relate to which levels of the expectations/outcomes?

2. What else does this piece show?

Next Steps

1. On the basis of what you see here, what would be your next specific teaching step for this student?

Figure 5.1 This annotation sheet can be used to add structure to the discussion when a sample of a student's work is shared with parents, other teachers, or other students.

task the student was doing. It is very hard to understand someone's work and its qualities without knowing what the student was asked to do or trying to do.

Question: How much support was provided, if any?

Unless the task was done under very strict test conditions, with no intervention at all by the class teacher or anyone else, you need to know whether or not the student was given any help. Such support should not be regarded as cheating; it was provided so that the student could show what he or she can do. There is absolutely no point – for the student, for the teacher, or for this kind of exercise – in giving students an exercise they cannot even start. If it is clear that the student is unable to get going on the task, then the teacher will provide help or move the student on.

Question: Why focus on the learning expectations/outcomes?

If the task has been designed to provide evidence of certain expectations/outcomes and standards, this issue is easy. If a teacher designed the task, it helps to know what to look for. Our scrutiny needs a focus – the learning expectations/outcomes.

Analysis

Question: Which characteristics of this work relate to which levels of the expectations/outcomes?

You are not being asked which level this single sample of work represents. It is not useful or valid, I believe, to derive the level of a student's achievement from one sample alone. You have to look at the work over a number of occasions to make a valid judgment. The purpose of this question, about the characteristics of the work compared to the criteria, is to look more closely and carefully at the detail of what the student has done. It may be that some aspects of the work are at one level and some at another. That is okay, as the overall judgment accommodates these variations and fluctuations from one piece of work to the next. For now, just identify, talk about, and record the characteristics or evidence for the criteria being looked at. Less-experienced teachers sometimes take longer with this than more-experienced ones. Give everyone a few minutes to look at the work on their own or in pairs before you launch into a whole-group discussion, to make sure that everyone is able to take part. It is interesting that some teachers have a very clear view about what constitutes "good writing" that makes no reference to the specific criteria they are meant to be using.

Question: What else does this piece show?

We can never pretend that everything important in a student's work is contained in the criteria laid down in a prescribed curriculum. Each student is unique, and we need to be constantly on the lookout for the cues and clues about how an individual student's mind is working. At this point, after looking for the things on the list of criteria, look for anything else that strikes you as relevant. Ask yourself: Is there anything interesting here, in the content, the expression, the presentation, the spelling, or the interpretation of the task that might need further checking or follow-up with the student?

> **Pause & Reflect**
>
> Why do you think it is useful to look for interesting aspects of a student's writing – beyond the required criteria?

The student's teacher may be able to help, or you may notice things that the teacher is just so used to and inadvertently overlooks.

Next Steps

Question: On the basis of what you see here, what would be your next specific teaching step for this student?

This question lies at the heart of teaching and learning. If we want to move this student's learning forward, what are the next one or two things we would need to do? These next steps are very intentional and functional. They are not of the "tell-the-student-to-try-harder" variety. A useful next step is, for example, to reteach or consolidate how students decide when to start a new paragraph, and to give some practice within the next few days, or to check whether the student understands when to use a capital letter or has just forgotten how to form upper- and lower-case letters.

It is a bit daunting to have other teachers discuss your students and their work and what you might do next. However, I have witnessed some very helpful and constructive conversations around this point, as more-experienced teachers share the strategies they have developed over the years, and the less-experienced teachers just soak up the information. Real teachers are given the opportunity to develop understanding by talking about practical ways of improving the learning of real students. These are topics that teachers need and want to talk about. With the right structure and opportunity, they do.

You may only get to look at two or three work samples during an hour-long meeting. That is fine, because the conversation has been about learning and teaching. When you have completed the annotation form for a work sample, pin the two together and keep them. They form the basis of a "standards portfolio," which can be of great benefit to teachers, school leaders responsible for the quality of teachers' judgments, the students, and the students' parents. Remember to keep all items in the portfolio anonymous.

Question: How does conversation between and among teachers help students' transition from year to year and phase to phase within and between schools?
The traditional groupings for teachers' conversation about learning and teaching in elementary schools relate to the age of the students: early-years teachers talk to other early-years teachers, Year/Grade 5 to others from Year/Grade 5, and so on. In some schools, however, these conversations have already moved on, examining "vertical threads" of learning progression through examples of students' work from different grade levels. The common ground for the conversations is provided by the age and stage of the students. In secondary schools, the common ground for teachers talking about learning and teaching is provided by the subject: teachers talk in departmental teams, about subject-related topics. It is often difficult for both sets of teachers to feel comfortable talking beyond these self-created boundaries, especially when a whiff of blame and defensiveness is in the air.

Conversations involving both elementary and secondary teachers that are based around analysis of student work bring special tensions of their own. To be successful, the conversation needs both a structure and some guidance, at least in its early stages. It also needs a rationale when teachers' time is short and other priorities are pressing. Sometimes, just to get things moving, the rationale has to be extrinsic. For example, it is expected in some school systems that teachers who use "level" in their calibration of students' progress will take steps to ensure that their interpretations of these levels are consistent. A further positive benefit is that teachers' greater clarity about expectations and progression will enable them to be clearer with their students in the day-to-day teaching.

In Canada and other countries where levels are particular to each grade, the first essential is that teachers within a grade level reach fair and consistent decisions about their students' learning when they report to parents and the school as a whole. To encourage teachers to see standardizing as both a vertical (across grade levels) and a horizontal (within a grade level) process, it may necessitate a wider view of each student's progress from year to year. Teachers first need to regard themselves as part of a team in which each member contributes to the learning and development of each student within the school. From this starting point, a teacher's interest and curiosity about what happens on either side of his or her particular grade level may increase, and need to be encouraged.

Some will no doubt argue that teachers working in vertical teams in the elementary school should, and do, start with planning. They start at the beginning and only later look at the outcomes of what the students have done. It sounds logical to do that, and quite illogical to work the other way round. My own experience of working with teachers tells me that starting at the end, with the students' work, and moving backwards into planning really helps to sharpen the mind. It also reduces the gap between the planning process and the classroom practice – between the rhetoric and the reality. Nothing is more engaging and stimulating for many teachers than seeing what the students actually do in the classroom.

Effective guidance of the teachers' conversations comes in many forms. For "random" thinkers like me, it is okay to jump back and forth between work analysis and planning as I begin to understand the connection between the two. Here is an example of how I have seen this happen.

A group of elementary-school teachers, in grades 5 and 6, were looking at some examples of students' written work. They started by reviewing the expectations of high-quality work as described in the provincial curriculum. Looking at the work itself, one or two of the teachers seemed disappointed that some of their students did not appear to have reached the highest standard. Their own experience with the students told them that they should have done so.

"Hang on a minute," said one of the teachers. "Let's go back to the task we actually set the kids to do. Did it really encourage them to show all they know and can do, or did the task itself put a limit on what they could show us?"

(cont'd. on next page)

Sure enough, the wording of the task and the way it had been presented to the students did not enable all of them to show the extent of what they could do. The link between task design and performance was becoming clearer. Then the teachers looked at the other end of the ability spectrum, and realized that the task did not enable students of more limited ability to show what they knew about writing in this mode either. If students with particular learning profiles had been restricted in this way by the task itself, could it be that the task was not enabling many students to do themselves justice? The teachers went "back to the drawing board" on task design and task presentation, and they learned really important lessons about designing assessment tasks that enable and encourage students to provide rich evidence of their learning.

When your discussion group includes teachers from different phases and schools, progress is understandably slower, because you will constantly come across things that some teachers take for granted and others do not. I remember elementary teachers with a special interest in language meeting with English teachers from the secondary school. We were looking at some students' writings about the books they had been reading. We noticed that in the secondary school the written work was based on the practice of having all the students in the class read the same book with their teacher. This observation led to the conversation below.

The elementary-school teachers looked at one another. "You mean you read the same text with all the kids?" one asked a secondary teacher.

"Yes, of course. What do you do?"

"We let the kids choose what they want to read, and then we set common written tasks based on each book," came the reply.

There was silence for a minute while we all thought about this. No wonder the kids are sometimes puzzled by what happens when they move from elementary to secondary school: we – the teachers – are puzzled ourselves. Things are not better, or worse – just very different from what we sometimes realize.

It is hard to anticipate all the issues that will arise when mixed groups of teachers look together at student work and analyze what it tells them about what has been learned and what is to come. Suffice to say that this focus has generated some of the richest and most interesting learning conversations between elementary and secondary teachers that I have witnessed.

Pause & Reflect

What types of tasks would help teachers from different schools to understand the others' approach to planning and finding evidence of student achievement? How might these conversations be organized?

I do not expect – and neither should you – that such conversations will produce instant enlightenment and the answer to all the challenges of trust, communication, and differentiation. With perseverance, though, all of these will definitely improve.

CHAPTER 6
The Heart of the Matter

In this chapter, we will focus on the last two bridges that support the successful transition of students from elementary to secondary school, and in particular, the teaching methods used in elementary and secondary classrooms. We will also look at the ways in which student learning and metacognition are promoted. As we have already noted, the final two bridges – the pedagogical and the learning-to-learn bridges, or groups of strategies – are central to the transition issue. According to research in the United Kingdom (UK), *these strategies are the most effective in promoting learning transition through the middle/junior-high years, but they are much less commonly found in existing practice.*

As we look at the strategies involved, we may understand the reasons for this gap between what is needed and what schools normally do. Both bridges include a complex mixture of habits and beliefs that have developed over many years. These may take a while to change – just as any other habits and beliefs do. People rarely feel comfortable doing something new for the first time. Once we are sure that these new strategies will lead to better student learning, the perseverance and practise will definitely pay dividends.

Bridge, or a "Rig"?

Although researchers use the term *bridge* to describe the strategies that support transition, at this point the metaphor is somewhat inaccurate. "Five bridges" seems to imply that each of the five is a separate entity that can be built independently of the others. For the first three bridges – the managerial, the social, and the curriculum content – that may well be true, and could be why schools have tackled them with some success. When we look at the last two bridges, however, it is quickly apparent that they cannot be built without the pre-existence of the first three. The following examples illustrate this complication:

- For teachers to fully understand the differences in approaches to teaching that exist between elementary and secondary classrooms, they really need to see each other at work. From my own experiences, I know that talking about teaching is never as effective as watching it happening, especially if we expect teachers to change some of their well-established practices. One hour's observation is worth many hours of meetings and rich conversations! The opportunity for observing, however, is a logistically complicated exercise. The teacher has to leave his or her classroom, travel to another school that has learners in a different "stage," and arrange to watch a colleague at work, paying proper respect to the professional protocols involved. Nor can the teacher just arrive unannounced at the other school and expect to be welcomed into another teacher's classroom. Further, arranging visits cost time and money. For watching to be effective, the logistics need to be properly managed. The principals from the participating schools need to encourage their staff to get involved, as well as to provide the necessary classroom coverage and time. Strategies involving managerial and bureaucratic arrangements are described as the first bridge. These links need to be in place before the fourth bridge – concerning the "how" of teaching and learning – is to be built.

- For students to become fully engaged and involved in "learning to learn," as described in the fifth bridge, the students need to feel safe enough to take some risks, tackle new ideas with confidence, and be prepared for self and peer critique. These conditions will not be met if students are feeling anxious about finding their way around the new building or wondering about how they fit in socially. Bridge five, therefore, depends on the pre-existence of social bridge two.

If we use the metaphor of a rig on which the most effective strategies for successful student transition can be built, then the three legs of the rig are strategies about management decisions, social needs, and curriculum content. It is essential, therefore, to realize that these first three bridges are necessary for successful transition, but they are not sufficient. Instead, they support the platform on which the two most important sets of strategies are constructed: the pedagogical bridge (the "how" of teaching) and the "learning-to-learn" bridge (improving students' metacognition and helping them develop how they see themselves as learners). On this platform, we can construct the edifice of a comprehensive transition program.

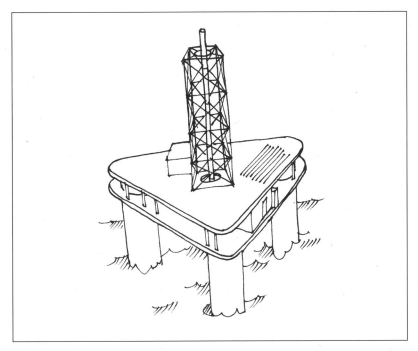

Figure 6.1 Three of the transition requirements – managerial, social, and curriculum content – are necessary but not sufficient for successful student transition. They need a *platform* to support the most important requirements – curriculum methodology and learning to learn.

The Pedagogical Bridge

In chapter 1, we looked at two teachers, both good professional practitioners. We considered their backgrounds, motivation and beliefs, and the circumstances of their daily work. Not surprisingly, their methods of teaching are different from each other. Not better or worse, just different. We also looked briefly at some of the experiences of two students at different stages in their learning lives. We saw the effects that different teaching and organizational practices had on them.

Pause & Reflect

- In what ways – other than the ages of the students – are teaching elementary-school students different from teaching secondary-school students?
- Where does your information about these differences come from? It could be from your own regular observations in a different stage of schooling, or – more likely – it could come from your memory of your own schooling, or the experiences of your children as they moved through the school system. How long is it since you observed students other than your own at work in a stage of schooling?

We have known for many years that major changes in teaching methods – the pedagogy or the "how" of teaching – can affect students' learning as they move from elementary school to secondary school. Teachers at different school stages plan differently, arrange teaching space differently, mark and assess student work differently, use different feedback procedures, write different styles of reports, emphasize and expect different things. Many students have the confidence to rise to these new expectations and ways of doing business and to ask questions, if necessary. Many others are less confident and resilient, confused by the variety of teachers and methods they encounter, and by the possible variety of practice from one teacher or department to the next. This is not to say that teachers are unhelpful. However, many students lack the confidence to ask questions when they are with peers who they may not yet know or trust. Teachers may assume that students are clear about expectations when, in fact, they are not but are afraid to say so.

We also know how important it is to pick up the learning threads from the students' prior experiences and get weaving as quickly and effectively as possible, making sure that prior learning is recognized and respected. When you do not know the new group of students well, it is all too easy to pitch your teaching challenge too low or too high, leaving students bored by the first and discouraged by the second. Boredom and discouragement can quickly lead to disengagement and low-level disruption by some students. Such behaviours can adversely affect the learning relationship between the teacher and the group. Both teachers and students gain much from planning teaching activities that are engaging and challenging, especially during the first weeks and months of secondary school.

Without warning or practice, students have to adapt their learning habits to their teachers' styles, and some will find this harder to do than others. Students in secondary classrooms often make fewer choices about how they work than they have been accustomed to making in their previous learning lives. Teachers may not even be aware of this. If they are, they might rationalize the approach as a "fresh start" in learning, paying little regard to their students' prior experiences or dismissing prior experiences as "childish."

In the elementary classroom, the teacher expected the students to find and use resources that she had arranged in various places around the room. The teacher also provided space for small-group· discussion and a quiet corner for students who wanted to work alone. Students were encouraged to get out of their seats to look for something they needed and to put it back afterwards.

In the secondary classroom, things were arranged differently. The teacher had the students' desks in rows facing the front, and she provided the necessary resources herself. Students were assigned various organizational tasks but under the teacher's direction. When a student got up without permission and took a book to a corner of the room to read, this behaviour was considered inappropriate and was challenged by the teacher.

As we search for strategies to help students adapt more successfully to the different teaching styles they may encounter in secondary school, it might be helpful to start with improving teachers' understanding of and respect for the different ways of working that their students will encounter.

Take the initiative to observe how teachers teach in different professional circumstances and settings. This is often all it takes to get teachers to think about the implications for students and useful strategies for ensuring a smoother learning progression for all students, not just the most confident and adaptable.

Not every teacher is able to or willing to participate in the above kinds of activities. Teachers who visit other classrooms, therefore, need time and encouragement to share what they have seen and learned with their colleagues. "Mutual classroom visitations" are not about teachers judging each other or finding reasons to blame each other. The purpose is to gather information about *students'* actual experiences, so teaching can be adapted to maximize their progression in effective learning.

Obviously, an important precondition of making such fact-finding strategies effective is the preparedness and open-mindedness of the teachers involved. This brings us back to the metaphor of the platform on which the most effective transition strategies can be built. Schools and their teachers need to decide whether or not fact finding is something they want and need to do – that is, is the focus on learning and teaching, or is it just on the social arrangements to help students

The grade 6 teacher was aware of how differently the secondary classroom would be run, and she explained this to her students before they moved on. She represented the change as a major challenge, telling her students that in secondary school they should not expect to get much help from the teacher. She also warned them that they might be punished if they approached their learning in the "big school" in the same way as they had been working in the elementary school. The students listened carefully to her. Some recognized the risks involved in change but felt that they would cope with it if they paid attention. Others felt that they would probably fail and end up in trouble pretty quickly. In some cases, this expectation did indeed contribute to the students floundering quite early on. This teacher was trying to help her students realize the differences they were about to face, but the unexpected consequences of her actions were not helpful for some of her students.

Pause & Reflect

What could the teacher in the above example have done differently to help her students prepare for possible changes ahead?

settle into their new environment? We have to believe that our students will learn more and learn faster when we try to reduce the number of learning blocks they face at transition. It is all too easy for teachers to feel defensive and/or blame each other for the perceived difficulties that students experience. Once the blaming starts, professional respect and trust can be damaged all too quickly, and it is much harder to start again. For this reason, I believe it is important to give careful thought before sending teachers to check out how students learn and teachers teach in other stages of schooling.

I overheard a receiving teacher comment along the following lines to a student, "Don't tell me this work is the best you can do, because we can both see that at the start of this work you were achieving more." It was now up to the student to acknowledge his own capabilities and make the necessary improvements.

In many elementary schools, teachers are encouraged to include a student's writing samples in the cumulative file that moves up the school as the student progresses. In the Comprehensive Assessment Program in Winnipeg schools, for example, detailed assessments and observations are conducted by the classroom teacher at the beginning of each school year. These samples of work provide a long view of students' progress

Something to Try

Below are some of the things that teachers who I have worked with and schools that I have worked at have done to understand each other better.

- Make arrangements for teachers to spend time working in a classroom where students are in the grade before or grade after the one the visiting teacher currently teaches. It may be harder to make this arrangement than it sounds because of the logistical complications, but with a clear purpose and encouragement from the respective principals it can convey a world of meaning in a short time and be a.real eye-opener. Teachers have told me how they have seen students a few months younger than those they usually teach behaving in quite different ways, making more decisions and taking more responsibility than they assumed they were capable of, and achieving at a level that was not seen again for quite a while after the transition. These teachers asked themselves why this might be so and how they could harness more effectively the learning energy of these students.
- Elementary school teachers may need to follow some secondary-school students around for half a day or so to get a clear idea of how teaching is affected when students move from one teacher and room to another – sometimes with the same peers, sometimes not. This is an effective way to view how the different teaching arrangements affect the students' engagement, behaviour, learning, and achievement. It is a salutary experience for secondary teachers to do this also, to see how the students they teach fare in other parts of the same school. When elementary teachers experience life in the "big school," they are then in a better position to help their students and students' families understand the changes they will be facing.
- Find a representative number of students, ask them some well-designed questions about their experiences as learners, and listen carefully to what they say. Some teachers worry about this way of gathering information. In my experience, however, when protocols are clearly explained, the students understand the questions and respond thoughtfully. If we want teachers to be curious about students' responses, teachers should compose the questions.
- When classroom visiting is too difficult to manage, use video recordings as a substitute. The results are not quite as illuminating as actually being in the classroom, but they are useful.

over time, and are of interest to the students and their families, as well as to the teacher.

For many teachers, getting a clear view of the previous work produced by students they are just beginning to teach is a challenge. The more we understand about our students' starting points, the more we

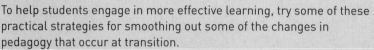

Something to Try

To help students engage in more effective learning, try some of these practical strategies for smoothing out some of the changes in pedagogy that occur at transition.

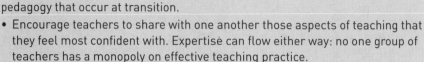

- Encourage teachers to share with one another those aspects of teaching that they feel most confident with. Expertise can flow either way: no one group of teachers has a monopoly on effective teaching practice.
- Arrange for teachers of a particular subject to look together at examples of student work on either side of the elementary/secondary "divide." This has a double benefit if it is handled well. First, teachers become more aware of one another's expectations and standards. Second, examination of student product can quickly lead to the question, "How did you get your students to produce work of this quality?" Talking together about the details of how teaching is organized to maximize learning and achievement is probably the most effective teacher discussion of all. Teacher discussions about pedagogies that do not have specific focus are sometimes too generalized to be useful. A shared focus on particular examples of students' work seems to provide a more productive starting point.
- For a few weeks before the students move to the next school, have them work in a special book or folder that they can take with them to the next school. The next teacher can then see at a glance what the students have been working on, how they approach their work, how assiduously they do or do not finish things off, the common errors they make, and particular talents they may be demonstrating. The receiving teacher, if he or she chooses, can use the books or folders as conversation starters with students about their work, as a means to help students differentiate the learning tasks and expectations, and as a benchmark to encourage the students toward higher standards.
- As well as providing very useful information to the receiving teacher, the books have a useful function for the providing teacher: during the last few weeks of the school year, students often lose interest in learning. For some students, the book will give them a focus that might not otherwise be there, and they will make a special effort with work that the next teacher is going to see.
- Examples of students' work from before the transition serve as a very useful reminder to both the students and their parents of the standards they are capable of achieving. These standards are not about comparisons with norms for the age group, but about student self-comparisons. Students who do not improve their learning at these transition times may be high-achieving students who have learned to do as much as their teacher expects – and no more. With a new teacher, when very high expectations may not yet have been established, the performance of these students may decline, not relative to the rest of the group but relative to their own previous best.

will need to differentiate our teaching, and most teachers recognize how hard it is to differentiate effectively all the time. We know what we have to do, but we may struggle to know how to do it.

We will not eliminate the gap altogether, but we can at least minimize or narrow it by planning lessons based on where the learners are at in our classrooms, not on where we think they should be.

The Impact of the Structures of Schooling

There is great variety from school district to school district, and even within a single district, about how to manage and organize the teaching of grade 6 through grade 10. As I mentioned in chapter 4, some elementary schools include students through to the end of grade 8 or grade 9. Other middle/junior-high graders are in middle/junior-high schools of two, three, or even four grade levels, and still others again start secondary school at grade 7, 8,

> **Pause & Reflect**
> - As teachers, we know that each student is unique. Can you think of two or three practical strategies that enable you to teach to each student's unique capabilities?
> - Is there any aspect of students' work or behaviour that might be particularly damaged by transition, and how might this be addressed?'

9, or 10. The practice, if not the content of teaching, is different in each of these environments, affected by the ways of doing business in the school as a whole. Students face different social challenges during the transition, depending on the age at which they change buildings and the size and composition of the student body they will join. In these varying circumstances, some general advice can be offered (and adapted to the existing structures of schooling).

My investigations in England and New Zealand suggest that both teaching and learning alter when the student no longer has the primary relationship with one teacher and moves on to several contacts with different teachers every day.

During the transition years of a student's learning life, there is a move away from a close relationship with one teacher to less-close relationships with more teachers. At this time, also, teachers in secondary schools encounter more students than do their colleagues in elementary schools.

At the same time, the students in their receiving school are working with other students that they do not know well. These new relationships, with both adults and peers, will be comfortable for more confident students and difficult for those who are less confident. The uncertainty will make some students less willing to take risks, which, in turn, adversely affects further learning.

The different circumstances of teaching affect teachers, too. For many teachers, less-intense relationships with their students (with fewer responsibilities) may be welcome.

The senior years of secondary school are more "high-stake" than the earlier years. In my experience as a secondary teacher in the UK, this sometimes means that teachers put more effort and energy into planning, feedback, and monitoring the older students, and have less focus on the younger ones. In some schools, too, there are more kudos and professional respect in teaching senior students, because the wider society seems to have greater respect for subject specialism and specialists. This can result in the allocation of less-skilled and less-experienced teachers to teaching the first grade level in secondary schools, to the possible detriment of those students.

Pause & Reflect

Do you think that teaching senior secondary-school students is as well respected as teaching younger students? If this difference exists, what are the implications?

Another important issue is: how many teachers should students be able to relate to? One suggestion is that students be encouraged to work with more adults and peers as they approach the end of their elementary education. Some argue that building learning relationships with more people better prepares students for secondary school. When students reach secondary school, the number of teachers that they have close contact with may need to be reduced, to ease them into this more complex learning environment.

Alternatively, the range of teachers may continue in the first year of secondary schooling, but students are assigned to an adult who keeps a much closer eye on them. For the first year, this adult can act as a substitute for the classroom teacher the students had in their final year of elementary, supporting them as they make the adjustment and transition to secondary school. In schools in England, this adult would probably be the "form tutor." Each tutor is given a group of 20 or so students and sees them at least once every day to check on how things are going, discuss learning collectively or individually, act as a first point of reference for parents and caregivers, and liaise with other teachers where and when necessary. The form tutor is the "learning monitor" for the students in his or her care. Some secondary teachers are initially uncomfortable in this role, regarding it as a distraction from their first duty to impart specialist knowledge. For other teachers, including me, the role of form tutor is one of the most satisfying parts of their career as a secondary teacher.

> **Pause & Reflect**
>
> In North American secondary schools, what are or could be the costs and benefits of ensuring that each student has a "teacher adviser" or homeroom teacher who can act as a learning mentor and monitor? What support or professional training would the teacher adviser need?

The "Learning-to-Learn" Bridge
Links with Assessment for Learning and "Self-Theories"

During the late 1990s, three separate and equally important research studies emerged. They were published without reference to one another, but all three have a bearing on successful student transition. The first was the Homerton College Cambridge team's focus on the underpinnings of student transition, which was published by the Education Ministry in England in 1999. One conclusion of this study was that students who understand themselves as learners make a more effective transition into secondary school than those who do not. The second research was pursued by Paul Black and Dylan Wiliam from King's College, London, who did a major meta-analysis of methods of assessment that most improve students' learning expectations/outcomes. They concluded, inter alia, that the quality of feedback and the engagement of students in self-reflection, peer critique, and feedback are major factors in improving students' achievement. Third, at about the same time, Carol Dweck from Columbia University in the United States published her book about "self-theories." Her research is based on many years of investigation into learners' mindsets and the impact of self-theories on learning success. Her work concludes that learners who have a positive

view of their own capability – the growth mindset – are more likely to
be successful than those who believe that their capacity is dependent
on factors they cannot control – the fixed mindset – such as genetics,
chance, or the behaviour of people other than themselves. From her
decades of investigation, Dweck concludes that the growth mindset can
be developed through effective feedback and learners' understanding or
awareness of their own progress over time.

The focus on developing the students' metacognition as a step toward
more successful transition is worthy of very special attention, for a
variety of reasons:

- Teaching strategies aimed at improved student metacognition can
  be used in age-appropriate ways throughout a student's learning
  life, providing a continuous pedagogical thread across the years of
  transition and aligning learning experiences for students.

- The metacognitively self-aware student becomes the "vehicle of his
  or her own learning/growth" at transition. Instead of relying solely
  on teachers to make learning links across the transition in schooling,
  students make their own connections, analyze the differences, and
  consider the implications and next steps needed to improve their
  learning progression. Before students transfer from one grade or level
  of schooling to the next, we involve them directly in considering how
  the coming changes may affect their learning and what they can do
  to help themselves. After the students have moved on, their receiving
  teachers continue to use self-reflection and peer-critique processes,
  and expect their students to help keep track of their own learning
  successes and challenges that they experience. Each student is now
  self-checking/monitoring and helping his or her peers, in addition to
  the teacher keeping track of the learning of the whole group.

- Students who are accustomed to keeping track of reflecting about
  and analyzing their own learning do a better job of communicating
  with and involving their parents and caregivers. These adults can
  be of great support to their children if they understand what the
  challenge of transition is all about. Without a focus on learning and
  classroom achievement, many families are, understandably, most
  concerned with social and behavioural aspects as their child
  moves on.

- The habits and practice of student involvement in keeping track of their own learning can be a very useful anchor during the changes in teaching and learning that take place during transition. It may be, however, that the rationale for these expectations will need to be explained to students and their families in slightly different terms on entry into the secondary-school environment. We have to remember that students regard entry into secondary school as an important rite of passage and part of growing up. We want them to continue to use and develop learning-to-learn skills they have developed in elementary school, not as a gesture toward past practice and continuity but as part of becoming an adult learner. As students enter secondary school, we talk to them about the learning skills they will need to be successful as learners while there and beyond. We discuss the importance of independent and inter-dependent learning, about identifying and applying specific success criteria to their work, about learning self-management. Basically, we are asking our students to think like teachers and be active participants in their own learning rather than passive recipients. In addition, and crucially, we share with both the students and their parents what we know about how active student learning improves grades and scores and consequent life-chances. Learning to learn is not a distraction from improving scores but an essential means to do so. Teachers need first to understand and act on this, and be willing to share this belief with the students and their families.

Teaching Strategies Designed to Support Learning to Learn

Many teachers in North America and elsewhere have been introduced in recent years to the key elements of assessment for learning. The strategies involved were summarized by the UK Assessment Reform Group in 1999 and serve as concise guidelines with far-reaching implications for the ways in which teachers, learners, and schools do business. In each of the five instance below, the statement is the precise wording chosen by the education researchers who gave us this list. Beneath each statement, I have added a more precise definition or implication to be considered.

1. The provision of effective feedback to students

   "Effective feedback" means descriptive, specific, related to clear criteria understood by the student, timely, and suggesting next steps. Teachers' marking and grading practices are the necessary starting point here.

2. The active involvement of students in their own learning

   Notice that student involvement includes their own learning, not just assessment. This has implications for pedagogy and the willingness and ability of teachers to engage their students at all stages in the learning cycle.

3. Adjusting teaching to take account of the results of assessment

   This can be done periodically after an assessment, to link the expectations/outcomes to future planned learning. It can also be done within a lesson, with teachers checking informally how well their students are learning, and adjusting their activities as a result. There are implications for teachers' approaches to planning. If the first goal of planning is content coverage, this degree of flexibility may be problematic. On the other hand, if the first goal of planning is student learning, there is no dilemma here.

4. Recognition of the profound influence assessment has on the motivation and self-esteem of students, both of which are crucial influences on learning

   All teachers understand the connection between students' motivation and improved student performance. The question is how best to motivate our students. This provides a clear link between the ALP research and the work of psychologists such as Carol Dweck. Motivation is the key to improved student performance.

5. The need for students to be able to assess themselves and understand how to improve

   Wording is crucial here. Before students are given the opportunity and encouragement to self and peer assess, we have to coach them thoroughly on how to do it and develop their skills through practice.

Pause & Reflect

From your professional reading and your experience, what do you feel are the most effective ways of enhancing students' motivation? If intrinsic motivation is the long-term goal, how can that best be developed during the years of schooling?

Assessment for Learning: Classroom Strategies
Scaffolding

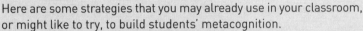

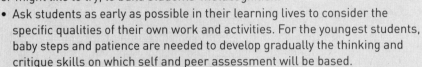

Something to Try

Here are some strategies that you may already use in your classroom, or might like to try, to build students' metacognition.

- Ask students as early as possible in their learning lives to consider the specific qualities of their own work and activities. For the youngest students, baby steps and patience are needed to develop gradually the thinking and critique skills on which self and peer assessment will be based.

- Offer students exemplars of work at various levels, and expect them to develop criteria or a rubric based on their perceptions and definitions of quality. Students will need a fair amount of guidance to start with. They will become more skilled and quicker with practice.

- Instead of giving students a complete rubric to guide their work, be prepared to take a little longer to improve students' understanding of the criteria. Offer students a partial rubric, and give them an opportunity to complete it by adding different aspects of success to be considered, rewording statements of quality, finding examples to illustrate different aspects of quality, or tweaking the original rubric to customize it for use. They will find it easier to complete a partial rubric than to start from scratch. Students could work in groups to arrange the samples in a progression of growth and explain why the sample is a beginning sample, one that is almost there, and one that best represents what is important about the work. This process is one that takes time in the beginning and needs to be repeated. As a result, it moves quicker as students experience and understand the process better. It has a huge impact on helping students self assess and provide meaningful feedback to their peers.

- Once criteria for quality work are clear to the students, offer them anonymous examples of work done by other students, and have them practise applying the criteria to these examples and considering the specific feedback that they could offer to improve the work. Students need to learn to separate feedback from friendship: starting them with anonymous examples of work for analysis will make peer assessment and feedback more effective later.

- Create an "imperfect sample," and suggest to students that they can help a peer get a better mark by letting him or her know which criteria have been met (or give two strengths) and which aspects still need to be worked on. Have students then suggest a next step that would strengthen the work.

- Use exemplars of work displayed in the classroom to encourage students to examine and compare these exemplars to their own work and decide where and what next to improve. Exemplars that represent standards are often more useful to clarify expectations and progress than statements about

(cont'd. on next page)

quality. Words have only limited meanings for many learners: seeing what is expected is more effective than hearing or reading about it – both for parents and students. Choose exemplars that enable students to see the progression from their current standard to higher ones. If the exemplars show work too far beyond the current capability of the students, they may find this very discouraging.

- Teach students about the workings of their own brains. Dweck's emphasis on developing a "growth mindset" includes helping students understand that their brains do grow and will grow given challenge and perseverance. Many parents also find this fascinating, as they may not have heard much about recent studies about how the human brain works, and what the implications are for learning.
- Encourage teachers to "plan for learning" rather than "plan for coverage," and give them time to adjust the hard-wired habits involved.
- In elementary classrooms, suggest that teachers start with developing more learning-focused approaches to planning, pedagogy, questioning and conversations, marking, and feedback in one area of learning before widening the scope. For secondary teachers, suggest they start with one teaching group to practise different approaches, and gradually widen the approach to other groups as new habits begin to replace older ones and teachers' confidence grows. In both cases, teachers need to see for themselves the impact on students' commitment, effort, and behaviour, as well as the effect on learning success. Teachers need to see benefits for themselves and for their students if these practices are to be truly sustainable.

In 2006, I was part of a team from Winnipeg School Division that published a series of books for teachers entitled, *Creating Independent Student Learners*. There are three books for teachers, aimed at nursery/kindergarten to grade 3, grades 4–6, and grades 7–9, and a book for school leaders concerning the implementation of these practices across the school. Becoming an independent learner is a major step for students' successful transition from elementary into secondary education – there is a clear overlap between the focus of those publications and the focus of this one.

Over several years' work with teachers and students in Winnipeg's Inner City School District, we developed the simplest possible suggested steps for teachers and schools aiming toward greater independence and metacognition of their student learners.

The eight steps, referred to as "The Scaffolding," are divided into three stages: Setting the Target, Practice, and Reflection.

1. Setting the Target

    Step 1: Understand the learning task and the learning intent.

    Step 2: Share task and intent with students, in accordance with their "learning profile." Discuss with the students: "What will the work look like when we finish? How will we know when we have met the target?"

    Step 3: Design and carry out "enabling tasks" that lead students toward the learning goal.

2. Practice

    Step 4: Provide a first attempt for the students to show what they know and can do.

    Step 5: Invite comparison, between what the student has done so far and the desired outcome.

    Step 6: Have students identify the next step.

    Step 7: Provide a second attempt to meet the chosen goals, using the chosen next step.

3. Reflection

    Step 8: Encourage the students to look back and reflect on themselves as learners.

The Transition Portfolio

When teachers and students have practised this way of working for a while, the students should be willing and able to present themselves as learners in student-led conferences, usually with parents as part of the reporting process. If student-led conferencing has been part of the students' life throughout the elementary years, by the time students approach the transition into secondary education, they should be ready to present themselves as learners. From this springs the idea of a "transition portfolio," generated by each student, through which students can illustrate their learning journey and aspirations. One of the audiences for such a presentation would be the next team of teachers who will encounter the student in the new learning environment.

Pause & Reflect

What are the technical, educational, and logistical challenges surrounding the idea of students' individual digital portfolio to share with the next school? What could be done to overcome or accommodate these challenges? How might we begin such a process to support creating a transition portfolio with students?

Students today and in future generations are and will be able to illustrate their learning in far more ways than those from previous generations were able to. They commonly have access to sophisticated equipment and possess the skills to capture images, edit them, and share them. Building an electronic portfolio is not difficult technically. The difficulty lies in helping students reflect deeply enough on their own learning, progress, talents, and goals, and to make good decisions about what to share and how to do so. The transition portfolio will show not only what the students have learned but also how self-aware they have become as learners.

As with many strategies for learning improvement, the idea of a transition portfolio is attractive, but "the devil lies in the detail." We need to consider the following:

- The time and support necessary for reflection and discussion about what to capture in the portfolio
- How students manage input during their final weeks or months in the elementary environment
- The willingness and capacity of the teachers in the secondary school to welcome, consider, and respect these offerings, and to take account of them when planning learning experiences for these students in the early weeks and months of their secondary schooling

I offer a note of caution here. A student portfolio not connected with reflections on learning could end up as a sophisticated digital extrapolation of the "social bridge" at transition. The information will be about personal or extra-curricular activities and will be viewed presumably by adults most concerned with the social integration and confidence of the incoming student. Like the other elements of the "social bridge," personal portfolios are important but not sufficient to overcome the barriers to learning at transition time. If a key purpose of the digital portfolio is for the student to represent and illustrate himself or herself as a *learner*, this should clearly affect the selection of material and the choice of audience. A portfolio, like any other form of communication, starts with clear decisions and common understandings about purpose and audience. All too often in current transition practice, the receiving teacher who needs the information does not receive it in the most effective and efficient way. It is important for all involved to understand (1) why the information is being gathered, (2) what could or should be its impact for improving learning, (3) who will be looking at it, and (4) what is being looked for. In order to achieve the purpose of sustaining and developing student learning, the structures, contents, and timing of a transition portfolio will need to be negotiated between the providing school, the receiving school, and the students themselves.

Pause & Reflect

- In the schooling structures and climate of your community or district, what might a learning transition portfolio contain?
- To achieve the transitional portfolio's purpose to develop learning during this period, how could the portfolio be managed before and after the student's transition?
- How might you begin the process of creating a transition portfolio with students?

Conclusion

From the voices of the students and the teachers, as well as the researchers, we have seen the importance of developing trust and effective liaison between the teachers and principals in our various schools and stages of learning. Trust can be built through contact and communication, but until a modicum is assured, the communication maybe difficult and fraught with misunderstandings and even resentment.

Communication, in person as well as on paper or electronic, can be time-consuming and frustrating. It is not easy to find agreement on the details, as well as on the broad principles. The communication needed here is not just about the students and their needs and achievement. To cross the pedagogy bridge, teachers need to communicate with each other, across the barriers of training and institutional habits. Within secondary schools, there is an urgent need for greater communication, also, to focus teachers on the learning of the students they share, beyond subject loyalty, which has been the main reference point for far too long.

Sound assessment practice implies a wealth of understanding about the purpose, strategies, and usefulness of assessment to a variety of audiences. When we hand on our students to the next stage in their learning lives, the information we gather about them must be as accurate, consistent, and fair as we can manage. When this information is received by the next team of teachers, it needs to be respected, understood, analyzed, and used thoughtfully to plan effective teaching for the receiving students.

Finally, I have some thoughts about differentiation, a clumsy word with infinite implications for the classroom teacher. It implies that we aim to provide teaching tailored to the individual needs of individual children, in all areas of their learning. The challenge to the elementary teacher is to keep all the learning plates spinning simultaneously for all the children, balancing science with music and technology and everything else, while still emphasizing the basics of numeracy and literacy. In the secondary school, most teachers see upwards of 100 students every week, and for some teachers it is many more. Their challenge is to treat each student as a unique learner, whose individual needs can and should be catered for. For most teachers, absolute differentiation is an impossible goal. All we can do is strive a little closer to it each year, and cope with the continuing feeling of dissatisfaction and frustration while, at the same time, we attempt to narrow the range of the gap that exists between learners.

Building the "learning-to-learn" strategies and sustaining them as students move from one school to another is one of the hardest, yet, most satisfying, aspects of education. As teachers, we need to keep our focus on the learning skills and needs of our students in today's world. Our students have to be resilient, reflective, self-aware, determined, and demanding, and we cannot allow the structural or cultural barriers between elementary- and secondary-school education distract them – or us. None of this will be possible, however, without some changes of practice and adoption of different approaches.

Making Plans, Taking Action, and Checking the Impact

Only you can decide how much of a priority the issue of transition is for you. You may have already gathered evidence that convinces you that too many of your students are struggling during their first year in their next-stage school. If so, you have to weigh this issue against the other priorities you have already agreed upon and built into your school development plans. It is imperative to remember, though, that improving your students' learning is a continuing core purpose – never an initiative – of your school and every other school, regardless of the grade level. You may be able to weave the strands of the issue into existing priorities rather than treat transition as something new and freestanding. If you decide that it will have to wait for a year or two, try to spend the intervening time gradually preparing the groundwork. As I have pointed out throughout this book, attitudes are a critical underpinning factor, and attitudes are the slowest to change. Therefore, it is never too early to think about and talk about this issue before the detailed plans are laid.

The complexity of transition demands a carefully thought-through plan. Keep the various necessary ingredients – trust, communication, sound assessment practice, differentiation – simmering simultaneously while you foster the connection between them all.

As you plan, consider, too, how you are going to check whether or not the action you take creates the effect you aspire to. This means including an evaluation strategy in your plan from the beginning, not tacking it on at the end as an afterthought. Ongoing periodic monitoring and evaluation will take time, and the resources you require will need to be factored into both your budget and your professional development goals.

In this concise resource, I have offered some strategies for achieving successful student transition from elementary to secondary schools in your community or your district. I encourage you to adapt these suggestions to meet your specific and unique circumstances.

References

Anderman, E. M., and M. L. Maehr. "Motivation and Schooling in the Middle Grades." *Review of Educational Research* Vol. 64, No. 2 (1994): 287–309.

Assessment Reform Group. *Assessment for Learning: Beyond the Black Box.* Cambridge, UK: School of Education, University of Cambridge, 1999.

Barber, M. "Bridges to Assist a Difficult Crossing." *Times Educational Supplement,* March 12th, 1999, <www.tes.co.uk/article.aspx?storycode=313443>.

Black, P., and D. Wiliam. "Assessment and Classroom Learning." *Assessment in Education: Principles, Policy & Practice* Vol.5, Iss.1 (1998): 7–74.

_____. *Inside the Black Box: Raising Standards Through Classroom Assessment.* London, UK: School of Education, King's College, 1998.

Clarke, P., T. Owens, and R. Sutton. Creating Independent Student Learners series. Winnipeg, MB: Portage & Main Press, 2006.

Dweck, C. *Mindset: The New Psychology of Success.* New York: Ballantine Books, 2008.

_____. *Self-Theories: Their Role in Motivation, Personality, and Development.* Philadelphia: Psychology Press, 1999.

Galton, M., J. Gray, and J. Rudduck. "The Impact of School Transition and Transfer on Pupils' Attitudes to Learning and Their Progress." *Research Report RR 131,* 1999.

Kirkpatrick, D. "What's the Point? Changes in Students' Beliefs About Academic Work in Transition From Primary School to Secondary School." *Set: Research Information for Teachers,* No. 1 (1997): 1.

Poskitt, J. Massey University, New Zealand, for the Assessment for Learning and Progression (ALP) Project, New Zealand Ministry of Education, 1998 and 1999.

Wigfield, A., et al. "Transitions During Early Adolescence: Changes in Children's Self-Esteem Across the Transition to Junior High School." *Developmental Psychology* 27 (1991): 552–565.

Wormeli, R. "Movin' Up to the Middle." *Education Leadership* Vol. 68, No. 7 (April 2011): 48–53.

Suggested Further Reading

A Google search will reveal a number of recent studies pertinent to schooling in Canada and the United States. The following titles provide additional connections between what we know about successful student transition and the need to promote student self-efficacy, motivation, and engagement in learning.

Absolum, M. *Clarity in the Classroom: Using Formative Assessment for Building Learning-Focused Relationships*. Winnipeg, MB: Portage & Main Press, 2010.

Brookhart, S. *How to Give Effective Feedback to Your Students*. Philadelphia: SCD, 2008.

Crooks, T. J. "The Impact of Classroom Evaluation Practices on Students." *Review of Educational Research* Vol. 58, No. 4. (1988): 438–481.

Flutter, J., et al. *Improving Learning: The Pupils' Agenda*. Cambridge, UK: Homerton Research Unit, 1999.

Hargreaves, L., and M. Galton. (eds.) *Moving From the Primary Classroom: Twenty Years On*. London, UK: Routledge, 1999.

Koechlin, C., and S. Zwaan. *Q Tasks: How to Empower Students to Ask Questions and Care About Answers*. Markham, ON: Pembroke Publishers, 2006.

Qualifications and Curriculum Authority. *Building Bridges*. London, UK: Qualifications and Curriculum Authority, 1997.

Rudduck, J., R. Chaplain, and G. Wallace. (eds.) *School Improvement: What Can Pupils Tell Us?* London, UK: David Fulton Publishers, 1996.

Sutton, R. *Primary to Secondary: Overcoming the Muddle in the Middle*. Salford, UK: Ruth Sutton Publications, 2000.